T5-BPZ-637

How Little is Enough? SALT and Security in the Long Run

Francis P. Hoeber

Foreword by Elmo R. Zumwalt, Jr.

Published by

Crane, Russak & Company, Inc.

New York

National Strategy Information Center, Inc.

How Little Is Enough? SALT
and Security in the Long Run

Published in the United States by

Crane, Russak & Company, Inc.
3 East 44th Street
New York, NY 10017

Copyright © 1981 National Strategy Information Center, Inc.
111 East 58th Street
New York, NY 10022

Library of Congress Cataloging in Publication Data

Hoeber, Francis P.
How little is enough?

(Strategy paper ; no. 35)
Includes bibliographical references.
1. United States—National security.   2. United
States—Military policy.   3. Strategic forces—United
States.   4. Strategic Arms Limitation Talks.   I. Title.
II. Series: Strategy papers ; no. 35.
UA23.H533   355'.033073   80-22777
ISBN 0-8448-1383-4 (pbk.)

Printed in the United States of America

How Little is Enough?

(

Contents

The author would like to acknowledge the support of the Earhart Foundation, Ann Arbor, Michigan in the preparation of this book.

Foreword

Elmo R. Zumwalt, Jr.
Admiral, U.S. Navy (Ret.)

Senate consideration of advice and consent to ratification of the grossly-inequitable and unverifiable SALT II Treaty has been indefinitely postponed, on the announced grounds of the Soviet invasion of Afghanistan. Even before the invasion, however, there was increasing doubt that approval of ratification could pass by the required two-thirds majority, because of growing concern with respect to: (1) the Treaty's defects, (2) the impending vulnerability of U.S. Intercontinental Ballistic Missiles (ICBMs) to a portion of the Soviet MIRVed SS-18 force, and (3) the overall Soviet strategic superiority foreseen for the early 1980s. Thus it would appear that by invading Afghanistan the Soviets gave President Carter a way out of what would probably have been an embarrassing political defeat.

However, the Soviet action in Afghanistan and the Senatorial concerns about the SALT II Treaty are not unrelated. It is precisely the Soviet strategic parity of the 1970s and their foreseeable superiority in the 1980s, or what the Soviets call the change in the "correlation of forces," that has emboldened them in the exercise of military adventurism.[1] The Soviets underwrote the breaking of the 1973 agreement for peace in Indochina; the Egyptian attack on Israel in 1973; the increasing violation of the 1962 agreements on Cuba and the gradual communist penetration, encirclement, and potential closing of the Caribbean; the campaign in Africa, beginning with the joint Soviet-Cuban penetration of Angola in 1975, the Soviet-Cuban support of Ethiopia against Somalia, and the acquisition of bases and the prepositioning of supplies on the northern and eastern coasts of the continent; the support of

---

[1] In Soviet parlance, the correlation of forces includes political and economic factors as well as military forces, but "the military strength of a state is by all means a decisive element of its position in the world." (A. Sergiyev, "Leninism on the Correlation of Forces as a Factor of International Relations," *International Affairs,* May 1975, p. 101.)

communist regimes encircling the Middle East oil reservoir of Japan, Europe, and increasingly the United States; the buildup of Soviet forces in Europe, despite the concurrent buildup on the China border; the active encouragement of anarchy in Iran and instability in Saudi Arabia, with the supporting threat of the Yemeni proxies; and, finally, the brutal and unabashed invasion of Afghanistan.

The style of these increasingly bold demonstrations of Soviet global power and ambitions in recent years has been in sharp contrast to the cautiousness of earlier Soviet probing and Moscow's willingness to back down in the postwar period from Stalin through Khrushchev, from Berlin to Cuba. Moreover, with the invasion of Afghanistan the Soviets moved to the direct use of their own forces in addition to (but not as replacements for) the use of Cuban and other proxies. The Soviet actions in Afghanistan also marked the first overt step taken to expand the Soviet sphere of influence beyond that tacitly agreed upon at the end of World War II and codified by NATO acceptance of the Helsinki Final Act in 1975.

Neither the advent of Soviet military superiority nor Moscow's demonstrated willingness to use it—and understanding of how to do so—was unforeseeable or unforeseen. A number of observers and analysts, including the author of this study and myself, warned in print of these possibilities throughout the 1970s. Strategic analysis in this country, however, has long been dominated by wishful thinking about the feasibility of a deterrence-only doctrine and the utility of such concepts as overkill, finite deterrence, assured destruction, sufficiency, the cost-effectiveness criterion, etc. Such thinking has been supported by the insistence of many Americans that the Soviets do in fact share our beliefs, despite both Soviet strategic writings to the contrary and their ongoing strategic offensive and defensive programs.

The consequence of this wishful thinking has been unilateral U.S. restraint—under the last four Presidents and accelerating under President Carter—in the acquisition and modernization of strategic forces. President Carter has cancelled or delayed the few initiatives underway when he took over in 1977: the B-1 bomber program was cancelled; the cruise missile, the cruise missile carrier, the Trident I and II Submarine Launched Ballistic Missiles (SLBMs), the Trident submarine, and the MX missile programs have been delayed; the Minuteman III missile production line was closed down; and the nonstrategic (but related) neutron bomb—more properly, the enhanced-radiation artillery shell—was indefinitely postponed, under the pressure of a Soviet-inspired propaganda campaign. At the political policy level, abrogation of the Mutual Defense Treaty with the Republic of China (on Taiwan) and the (postponed) threat to withdraw U.S. ground troops from the Republic of Korea cast doubt on American constancy, further destabilized Northeast Asia, and may have weakened nonproliferation incentives. All these actions were taken in the name of detente and on the rationale that restraint would induce reciprocation by the Soviets and improve the prospects for SALT II.

It has not worked that way, but the dream of disarmament via SALT persists. The United States is still unilaterally observing the terms of the five-year SALT I Interim Agreement that expired in October 1977 and the unratified SALT II Treaty signed on June 18, 1979. SALT (and the Threshold Test Ban Treaty) has tended to inhibit U.S. national defense preparations far more than it has inhibited those of the Soviet Union. As is discussed in this study, this trend has been particularly apparent in the rates of buildup and modernization of the strategic forces of the two states, and in particular in the rates of improvement of accuracy.[2] Even the Antiballistic Missile (ABM) Treaty of 1972 has inhibited the United States more than the Soviet Union. In 1975, the United States decided unilaterally to dismantle the one ABM site permitted the U.S. under the 1974 Protocol, and American ABM research and development has proceeded at a fraction of the level undertaken in the Soviet Union.

A unilateral U.S. statement in 1972 asserted that failure to sign a permanent treaty on strategic offensive arms by the time of expiration of the Interim Agreement in 1977 would be considered grounds for abrogation of the ABM Treaty (which is subject to joint review every five years and provides for abrogation with six months notice by either side if it finds its supreme national interests to be jeopardized). Francis P. Hoeber and his close colleague, Amoretta M. Hoeber, proposed in January 1977 (in the *Armed Forces Journal*) that the new Administration consider abrogation if a treaty could not be reached by the expiration of the Interim Agreement.

It can be expected that the Reagan Administration will encounter

---

[2]In August of 1970, the Senate attached an amendment, sponsored by Senator Brooke, to a Fiscal Year 1971 military appropriations bill. This amendment restricted improvements in the accuracy of MIRVed missiles. See *Congressional Record*, August 27, 1970, p. 30253.

continued pressure from many participants in U.S. military and
foreign policy debates for the pursuit of nuclear arms reduction as an end
in itself rather than as an integral part of policies designed to enhance
national security. For this reason, Mr. Hoeber has undertaken this brief
but tightly-reasoned analysis of the risks and possible consequences of
future continuation, by any Administration, of a SALT "process" that
seeks bilateral reductions in strategic forces without due attention to:

(1) The need for adequate strategic forces to support the defense of
    U.S. vital interests and the containment of Soviet expansionism;
    and

(2) The role of strategic defenses and the increasing possibility that
    the United States will face the horrendous choice between deter-
    rence failure and appeasement/isolation/surrender of vital in-
    terests.

However, if the bad news of recent years has been that the United
States must pay the geopolitical price for the inadequate defense budgets
of the 1970s adhered to at a time when Soviet defense expenditures have
been steadily growing, the good news is that 1980 is seeing the development of a U.S. public consensus that the United States should
restore the military underpinnings of a foreign policy that can protect the
U.S. and the Free World. Opinion polls and my own dialogue with a
wide spectrum of audiences, ranging from groups on college campuses
to professional organizations, show that a majority recognize that the
United States no longer has military superiority over the Soviet Union,
and that a majority believes that we should restore the draft and increase
military spending. Even Senator Edward Kennedy has deplored the
Navy's recent report to Congress that it has a one-and-a-half-ocean navy
available to fight a three-ocean war. Since the 1980 presidential elec-
tions, it has become clear that the American people—and, increasingly,
their Congress—want to reverse the downtrend in American power
before it is too late. If this is to be accomplished at this late date, it is
important that the community of defense experts enrich the debate with
careful studies of the objectives, strategies, ways, and means of achieving such a reversal.

Mr. Hoeber has written elsewhere about the military balance and the
requirements for U.S. strategic forces. In this monograph, he probes
deeply into the relationship between U.S. arms control policies and

these strategic requirements, including the doctrine governing the use of strategic forces. He recommends the development and adoption of more rigorous arms control objectives, and suggests approaches to negotiation with the Soviet Union, the other nuclear powers, and U.S. allies. He has produced a useful contribution to the most important national debate of our time, and it should be widely read.

Executive Summary

Francis P. Hoeber in *How Little is Enough? SALT and Security in the Long Run* engages in an assessment of the rewards and risks of potential bilateral reductions—through the Strategic Arms Limitation Talks (SALT) or other arms control forums—of the levels of the strategic forces of the two superpowers. The monograph is not a search for precise numerical answers to the question "how little is enough?", but aims rather to "initiate a search for some guidelines for negotiations toward lower bilateral strategic arms levels," taking into account a number of political and military factors. At the core of Hoeber's analysis is his emphasis on the fact that no matter how attractive and compelling the goals of arms control may seem when viewed alone, arms control policies must not be formulated and considered in isolation; it is imperative that SALT and other arms control efforts be carefully related to such key dimensions of security as U.S. strategic (and conventional) requirements, doctrines governing the use of forces, and the complexities of the global strategic balance.

In analyzing these relationships, the author shows that the implications for U.S. security of current and possible future attempts to reduce strategic force levels must be assessed within the context of existing asymmetries in U.S. and Soviet strategic postures and doctrines. For example, implementation of the SALT II Treaty—far from enhancing U.S. security—would in fact perpetuate and even codify a lack of symmetry in the inventories and characteristics of offensive weapons, leading to a possible Soviet first-strike advantage. Furthermore, while U.S. strategic defenses are virtually non-existent, the Soviets have an elaborate program of both active and passive strategic defensive systems, including massive deployments in air defenses, operational strategic antisatellite defenses, and an extensive civil defense program. The fundamental differences between the U.S. deterrence-only and Soviet war-winning doctrines must be taken into account as well. As Hoeber points out, "The United States is a status quo nation and its military philosophy is one of deterrence, not of war-fighting. . . . The

Soviet Union, in contrast, is a still-expansionist nation with a philosophy of inducing change, by diplomacy where feasible, but by war as 'an extension of diplomacy' where necessary.''

Through the course of this monograph it becomes evident that significant reductions in strategic nuclear forces will entail many complex problems and potential pitfalls. Some bilateral strategic force reductions may be feasible *if they can be achieved equitably and verifiably,* Hoeber argues, but large reductions may have the net effect of lessening security by weakening deterrence and exposing the United States to intolerable risks. Deep bilateral cuts may further one goal of arms control, i.e., limiting worldwide damage should deterrence fail, but ''. . . if they go too deep, such cuts will actually weaken the more important arms control objective of preventing nuclear and major conventional war, as well as undue concessions of national interest to avoid war.''

Even if the U.S. and the Soviet Union were to achieve an *equitable* balance of strategic force levels, vastly reduced numbers would involve a number of long-range implications which might prove counterproductive to U.S. interests. For example, under a very low level of strategic forces:

1) The balance between the superpowers can be more easily destabilized by technological surprise, evasion, avoidance of limitations, and sudden breakout from the Antiballistic Missile (ABM) Treaty or other subsequently negotiated limitations on defenses.

2) Both active and passive defenses may become more effective, increasing the Soviet advantage in this area.

3) The power discrepancy between the superpowers and the other nuclear nations will be diminished, which may encourage these states to engage in a destabilizing buildup of their nuclear arsenals. Countries which presently do not have nuclear weapons may find the disincentives to nuclear proliferation decreased.

4) Reduced nuclear arsenals may ''make the world safer for conventional war,'' possibly necessitating an economically and politically burdensome buildup of U.S. conventional forces.

5) A shrinking U.S. strategic nuclear ''umbrella'' will weaken alliance cohesion and increase the likelihood of diplomatic coercion of the United States.

With these risks in mind, Hoeber suggests a number of guidelines for future arms control negotiations and military planning under hypothetical conditions of sharply decreased U.S. and Soviet strategic forces. At lower strategic levels it will become imperative to expand the domain of SALT to cover non-Central Systems, including some "Gray-Area" weapons (which are currently excluded), but also broadening negotiations to merge with other non-strategic arms control forums, notably the Mutual and Balanced Force Reduction (MBFR) talks in Europe. In such circumstances more parameters of strategic forces must be brought under control (e.g., throwweight, numbers of weapons rather than launchers only, and defensive as well as offensive armaments), and verification procedures must be strengthened. High force survivability will be crucial, and enhancing and ensuring the capabilities of much-reduced forces in such areas as reload/recycle capacities; accuracy; reconnaissance; and command, control, communications, and intelligence (C^3I) will become of increasing importance to U.S. security.

The author concludes by setting forth some precautionary unilateral measures that should be taken by the United States, whatever the pace of negotiated strategic force limitations, to maintain a credible deterrent and effectively protect·its interests around the world. For example, the U.S. should rebuild its air defenses, undertake a program of civil defense, and intensify its research and development activities in a number of areas. More serious attention must be paid to redressing the imbalance between the U.S. deterrence-only and Soviet war-fighting doctrines. In general, U.S. military power relative to that of the Soviet Union must be restored and maintained, for the cohesion of U.S. alliances and the security of the United States and the Western world.

Hoeber demonstrates that the problem of finding numerical answers to the question "how little is enough?" proves as intractable as answering the question of the 1960s, "how much is enough?" What does emerge quite clearly from this monograph is the advisability of great caution and careful study of the implications of going too rapidly down the road of massive strategic reductions, should the Soviets agree—for ingenuous or disingenuous reasons—to pursue this goal.

Glossary

ABM	Antiballistic Missile
ACDA	Arms Control and Disarmament Agency
ASAT	Antisatellite
ASW	Antisubmarine Warfare
C^3I	Command, Control, Communications, and Intelligence
Central Systems	Heavy Bombers, ICBMs, and SLBMs
Counterforce	An attack focused upon an enemy's military forces, particularly, although not exclusively, his strategic nuclear forces
CTB	Comprehensive Test Ban Treaty
DCPA	Defense Civil Preparedness Agency
FEMA	Federal Emergency Management Agency
FPA	Federal Preparedness Agency
GCD	General and Complete Disarmament
Gray-Area Systems	Weapons systems that are not classified as central systems per se, yet have strategic capabilities (i.e., the Soviet Backfire bomber, U.S. forward based FB-111s)
HE	High Explosive
HEL	High-energy Laser
ICBM	Intercontinental Ballistic Missile
IRBM	Intermediate Range Ballistic Missile
LNO	Limited Nuclear Options
MAD	Mutual Assured Destruction
MAP	Multiple Aim-Point
MBFR	Mutual and Balanced Force Reductions
MIRV	Multiple Independently-targeted Reentry Vehicles
MLBM	Modern Large Ballistic Missile
MPS	Multiple Protective Shelter
MX	Missile Experimental
NATO	North Atlantic Treaty Organization
Neutron Bomb	An enhanced-radiation warhead, designed to maximize radiation and minimize blast effects
OMT	Other Military Targets (not strategic nuclear forces)
R&D	Research and Development

RV	Reentry Vehicle
SALA	Strategic Arms Limitation Agreement
SALT	Strategic Arms Limitation Talks
SALT I	The series of negotiations beginning in the late 1960s resulting in the "Interim Agreement Between the United States of America and the Union of Soviet Socialist Republics on Certain Measures With Respect to the Limitation of Strategic Offensive Arms" and the "Treaty Between the United States of America and the Union of Soviet Socialist Republics on the Limitation of Anti-Ballistic Missile Systems," signed at Moscow on May 26, 1972
SALT II	The negotiations since SALT I, culminating in the signing on June 18, 1979, in Vienna, of the "Treaty Between the Union of Soviet Socialist Republics and the United States of America on the Limitation of Strategic Offensive Arms" and the "Protocol to the Treaty Between the Union of Soviet Socialist Republics and the United States of America on the Limitation of Strategic Offensive Arms"
SAM	Surface-to-Air Missile
SLBM	Submarine Launched Ballistic Missile
SRF	Secure Reserve Force
Throwweight	The useful weight which is placed on a trajectory toward the target by the boost stages of a missile
TRIAD	Combined strategic offensive force concept including ICBMs, SLBMs, and heavy bombers

Introduction

In Isaiah's mountain of the Lord's house, nations "shall beat their swords into plowshares, and their spears into pruninghooks." To many of his host of readers, Isaiah seems to imply that swords and spears are not productive, but plowshares and pruninghooks are. However, Isaiah specifically referred to days to come, when "nation shall not lift up sword against nation, nor shall they learn war anymore." Yet those days have not come, and nation still does lift up sword against nation.

The utopia of a disarmed world has eluded civilization since the Old Testament, but the concept has not died. The phrase "general and complete disarmament" (GCD) has been a Soviet slogan for over twenty years, and the United States has found it as hard to disagree with as motherhood.[1] Indeed, the name of the Arms Control and Disarmament Agency (ACDA) was a compromise in 1961 between those who wanted to increase national and world security by *control* of arms and those who saw arms control as meaningless without *disarmament*, (i.e., the reduction and eventual elimination of arms).

The difficulties of pursuing the chimera of GCD were clear in the 1960s, however. A more practical initial focus on nuclear weapons was agreed upon, and the concept of SALT—the strategic arms limitation talks—was formulated under President Johnson. ("Strategic" in this context means "strategic nuclear weapons."[2])

The 1968 Soviet invasion of Czechoslovakia postponed the initiation of the talks until the first year of the Nixon Administration. The "SALT I" talks started in the Fall of 1969 and culminated in the May 1972 Antiballistic Missile (ABM) Treaty and Interim Agreement on Strategic Offensive Arms. The long-term goal of GCD was reaffirmed at the time in a joint "Declaration of Principles," as follows:[3]

SIXTH. The parties will continue their efforts to limit armaments on a bilateral as well as on a multilateral basis. They will continue to make special

An earlier and shorter version of this essay appeared in *International Security*, Vol. 3, No. 3, Winter 1978/79.

1

efforts to limit strategic armaments. Whenever possible, they will conclude concrete agreements aimed at achieving these purposes.

The U.S.A. and the U.S.S.R. regard as the ultimate objective of their efforts the achievement of general and complete disarmament and the establishment of an effective system of international security in accordance with the purposes and principles of the United Nations.

In the "Joint U.S. and Soviet Statement on Strategic Offensive Arms," President Ford and Chairman Brezhnev, at Vladivostok on November 24, 1974, more cautiously indicated that "the new agreement will include a provision for further negotiations beginning no later than 1980–1981 on the question of further limitations and possible reductions of strategic arms in the period after 1985."

President Carter, however, has reemphasized the objective in SALT of eliminating strategic weapons. Shortly before he took office, he called for a study of the feasibility of reliance on some 200 to 250 strategic nuclear delivery vehicles.[4] In his Inaugural Address, he also stated an ultimate goal of a world free from nuclear weapons: "We pledge perseverence and wisdom in our efforts to limit the world's armaments to those necessary for each nation's own domestic safety. We will move this year a step toward our ultimate goal—the elimination of all nuclear weapons from this earth." His March 1977 SALT II proposals included a 10 to 25 percent reduction from the 1974 "Vladivostok Guidelines" limit of 2,400 intercontinental weapons launchers.

While President Carter's statements were widely discounted as simply rhetoric, or "looking at all options," it has become clear that the thrust of his thinking is firmly toward a return to a doctrine of finite or even minimum deterrence. Numerous Presidential decisions have unilaterally limited U.S. strategic capabilities and hedges: the cancellation of the B-1 bomber; the closing of the Minuteman III production line; the postponement of the MX missile; the delay in the cruise missile; the May 1977 concessions in SALT II after the "comprehensive" U.S. proposals offered in March; and the President's decision to continue to abide by the terms of the expired SALT I Interim Agreement and the negotiated but not ratified SALT II Treaty, when the Soviet invasion of Afghanistan (and the apparent lack of 67 votes to approve ratification) led him to postpone indefinitely Senate floor debate on the Treaty. The awkwardly handled decision to postpone the "neutron bomb," or enhanced-radiation shell, may have weakened deterrence at the substrategic level (which interacts with the strategic), and it certainly strained NATO alliance cohesion. Secretary of Defense Brown's first "Posture Statement" indicated a return to the McNamara concept of Assured Destruction and the capability to destroy 200 Soviet cities as a deterrent, while retaining some of the concept of flexible response and essential equivalence.[5]

The impact of the finite deterrence doctrine and its possible embodiment in SALT agreements must, therefore, be taken seriously and rigorously questioned. The implications of this doctrine for U.S. security may prove to be the most important issue facing this country in the 1980s, if actual military conflict with the Soviets is avoided.

Finite deterrence was first defined as official U.S. strategic doctrine by Secretary of Defense McNamara in the early 1960s. McNamara had flirted initially with a "city-avoidance, counterforce-only" doctrine.[6] This proposal evoked widespread protest, particularly from the Soviet Union, that it would make otherwise unthinkable nuclear war thinkable and hence more likely. Perhaps of greater impact in changing the Secretary's policy were the seemingly endless demands of his military technicians for both qualitative and quantitative increases in strategic arms to carry out the difficult—at that time almost impossible—counterforce mission with high confidence. McNamara's systems analysts therefore asked, "How much is enough?"[7] Their answer came in the doctrine of Assured Destruction. In this concept, the United States would require, and need not exceed, forces at a level sufficient—even after the absorption of a counterforce first strike—to inflict an arbitrarily-determined level of "unacceptable damage" on the Soviet Union.[8] The resources required for this task would be finite and manageable, and technological improvements, such as increased accuracy, would not be required. The Soviet Union would be deterred by the threat of "Assured Destruction."[9]

To be sure, the declaratory statements of U.S. strategic doctrine have evolved considerably since McNamara left office. In the period 1971 to 1973, President Nixon introduced the notion of *sufficiency,* including the concept of developing and maintaining the *flexibility* to respond proportionately and appropriately to—and thus to deter—a wide range of limited (i.e., less than "all-out") attacks. Secretary of Defense Laird in his posture statement for fiscal year 1973 added the term Realistic

Deterrence, to imply a broader concept of "total force" that included conventional as well as nuclear capabilities, with the aim "to discourage—and eventually to eliminate—the use of military force as a means by which one nation seeks to impose its will upon another. It seeks to deter war, but insures [sic] adequate capabilities to protect our nation and its interests should deterrence fail."[10]

Secretary of Defense Schlesinger in 1974 described the rationale for limited nuclear options,[11] thus giving more specific meaning to the concept of flexibility, while retaining the concept of Assured Destruction and "the avoidance of any combination of forces that could be taken as an effort to acquire the ability to execute a first strike disarming attack against the U.S.S.R."[12] During his tenure, Schlesinger also introduced the concept of an enduring reserve force for the Assured Destruction mission and began the shift from urban industrial targeting (including population) to economic and political targeting that eventuated in Secretary Rumsfeld's use of the term Assured Retaliation in lieu of Assured Destruction.[13]

In the following year, Rumsfeld further spelled out Assured Retaliation "as the effort to prevent or retard an enemy's military, political, and economic recovery from a nuclear exchange. Specific military forces and industries would be targeted. The effectiveness of the retaliation would be measured in two ways.

—by the size and the composition of the enemy's military capabilities surviving for postwar use;
—by his ability to recover politically and economically from the exchange."[14]

Secretary Brown continued to utilize the concepts of flexibility and essential equivalence, but also repeated that "It is essential that we retain the capability at all times to inflict an unacceptable level of damage on the Soviet Union, including destruction of a minimum of 200 major Soviet cities."[15] In the last two years, Secretary Brown has introduced the concept of a Countervailing Strategy. In this concept Secretary Brown has reiterated the need for flexibility; has given greater emphasis than in the past to the need for an enduring strategic reserve force (SRF), including the required command, control, communications, and intelligence (C^3I) capabilities; and has repeated that "because nuclear weapons also have political significance, we must maintain actual and perceived equivalence with Soviet strategic nuclear forces.''[16] Nevertheless, he also states that to achieve the deterrence objective ''we need, *first of all,* a survivable and enduring retaliatory capability to devastate the industry and the cities of the Soviet Union.''[17] (Emphasis added.)

We conclude, therefore, that—despite the evolution and refinements in the U.S. strategic doctrine over the past decade or more—the concept of Assured Destruction lives, by whatever name. Actual and perceived equivalence is an inherent objective in SALT negotiations. Assured Destruction, however, may not be possible at reduced levels of strategic arms; a secure strategic reserve force, not yet achieved, may become more difficult with progressive SALT reductions.

It is the object of this paper to initiate a search for some guidelines for negotiations toward lower bilateral strategic arms levels. We ask, in short, ''How little is enough?'' President Carter and many others believe that the ultimate answer should be ''zero nuclear weapons.'' There is great romantic appeal in this notion. However, even if we could get there from here—which we cannot—most people would have second thoughts about the desirability of this development, in view of the more than three past decades of peace among all nuclear powers and the fact that the horrors of a non-nuclear World War III would be rendered more likely in the absence of nuclear deterrence.

We will focus, therefore, on the less utopian but more practical question of the potential reduction, through SALT, of the levels of the nuclear arsenals of the two superpowers—arsenals which today overwhelmingly dominate those of the four or five other nuclear powers.[18] We do not evaluate herein the process of SALT and whether or not it is beneficial to the United States. We simply address a series of questions that will arise if the SALT process does continue, in pursuit of the objectives just stated.

How low can the two arsenals go and still permit the retention of a stable power balance? What are the risks and rewards of bilateral reductions? How, and at what levels, can these risks and rewards be balanced? What U.S. strategies, military and diplomatic (including in SALT), do the answers suggest? Given the yearning for escape from nuclear threats and the Administration policy of pursuing decreases under SALT, what conclusions can we reach on how much SALT is safe? Even things one believes good for the health must be taken in nonfatal doses.[19]

It is generally agreed that small decreases from the 1974 Vladivostok Guidelines levels, or from current levels (U.S. forces being somewhat below the Vladivostok 2,400 strategic nuclear delivery vehicles[20] and Soviet forces being somewhat above), would *not* have a serious effect on deterrence, one way or the other. The U.S. proposed a SALT II level of 2,160 (a ten percent reduction from Vladivostok), while the Soviets proposed a figure of 2,250 (a 6¼ percent reduction); disagreements in negotiating the SALT II Treaty had to do with what specific systems might have to be abandoned, not really with overall levels of forces or of deterrence. On the other hand, there is increasing recognition (for reasons that will become evident below) that retention of only 200 to 250 delivery vehicles would constitute a dangerously low level. The question is, can we determine a number in between that would be acceptable and one that would not? How little is *too* little?

Clearly, we shall not be able to determine precise numerical answers, but important principles that should govern the ultimate answer can be indicated. We shall first discuss existing U.S.-Soviet asymmetries and the deterrent threats that the United States may be able to pose at various levels of nuclear forces. The question of acceptable levels is sensitive to a number of both military and politico-military factors, which will then be considered. Finally, some hypotheses will be stated and some conclusions for policy will be drawn.

U.S.-Soviet Strategic Asymmetries and Their Roots

Before we can address the questions raised in the above introduction, we must ask where we stand today, and why. The SALT II Treaty—signed by President Carter and Chairman Brezhnev on June 18, 1979 and approved by the Senate Foreign Relations Committee on November 19, 1979, but not brought before the full Senate for a vote on approval of ratification because of the Soviet invasion of Afghanistan[21]—provides for nominal equality in strategic offensive forces. Equality, however, is established in terms of numbers of permitted strategic launchers. This category includes silos for ICBMs, submarine launch tubes for SLBMs, and heavy bombers, without any definition of the difference between heavy bombers and medium bombers (which are excluded).[22] There are also limits on the number of missiles which can be MIRVed (i.e., provided with Multiple Independently-targeted Re-entry Vehicles), on the number of bombers which can carry cruise missiles, and on the number of MIRVs or cruise missiles that can be put on a given type of delivery vehicle.[23]

Yet there exist gross asymmetries in the strategic postures of the United States and the Soviet Union, and in their strategic doctrines as well. Much attention has been focused on the fact that under the terms of the SALT II Treaty the Soviet Union is permitted far greater "throwweight" on its ICBMs (by a factor of between 4½ and 5 to 1), and in particular that the Soviets are permitted 308 "modern large ballistic missiles" (the SS-18, with about 15,000 pounds of throwweight), while the United States is permitted none (the maximum weight of a U.S. missile being that of its largest light ballistic missile, with 8,000 pounds of throwweight). The significance of this for the period of the Treaty, the early 1980s, is that a portion of the SS-18s, with 10 MIRVed warheads each and accuracy now estimated to be equal to that of U.S. missiles,[24] could eliminate up to 90 percent of the U.S. Minuteman and Titan II missiles in a first strike.[25] As Secretary of Defense Brown has stated, "For planning purposes, therefore, we must assume that the ICBM leg of our TRIAD could be destroyed within a very short time as one result of a Soviet surprise attack."[26]

There are other gross asymmetries as well. First, the Soviets have large numbers of medium-range bombers, capable of reaching the United States with refueling (which is required even for most heavy bomber missions). Secondly, the Treaty does not cover the production of missiles. Both sides produce extra missiles for testing (for proof of operational reliability and for training), but the Soviets have three active ICBM production lines while the United States has closed down its last Minuteman III production line. We cannot know how many missiles are produced in the closed Soviet society. Estimates of existing Soviet standby missiles have ranged as high as several thousand. (The United States has about 250).[27] Such missiles could be launched by many means, including from "soft" launchers (i.e., not silos) which could be concealed, even in missile-producing factories or missile-storage warehouses.

However, even if there were perfect symmetry in the inventories and characteristics of offensive weapons, and no first-strike advantage existed, there would remain great asymmetries in defenses. Let us consider defenses in two categories, active (weaponry) and passive (natural or artificial characteristics of targets).

Active Defenses

The first category of active defenses is comprised of the counterforce use of ICBMs (and potentially, in the future, SLBMs), primarily against the ICBM silos of the other side. In this connection, we already have noted the Soviet capability against the U.S. ICBMs and the lack of a corresponding Minuteman capability against the Soviet arsenal.

Under the terms of the 1972 Antiballistic Missile (ABM) Treaty, the U.S. and the USSR each were allowed two ABM sites with 100 missiles at each location, but all other terminal defenses against missiles were prohibited. The number of allowed sites was subsequently reduced to one each in the 1974 Protocol, and the one U.S. site (at Grand Forks, North Dakota) was dismantled by Congressional decision in 1975. We must also note, however, that the Soviets have pursued a much more extended and better-funded Research and Development (R&D) program since 1972, and the possibility of a Soviet breakout from the ABM Treaty, which could not be quickly matched by the United States, cannot be completely discounted.

In air defenses, the Soviets have massive deployments: surface-to-air missile (SAM) launchers, 12,000 SAMs, 2,600 interceptors, and an undetermined, or unpublished, number of radar-controlled antiaircraft cannon.[28] The United States, after the signing of the ABM Treaty, reasoned that air defenses were meaningless without defense against missiles, and therefore dismantled all but a token force of obsolete interceptor squadrons (327 interceptors) for "control of the sovereign airspace" in peacetime.[29]

Antisatellite (ASAT) defenses—i.e., weapons that can destroy satellites required for warning, intelligence, and command-control in wartime—have been operational in the Soviet Union for several years. An R&D program has been initiated in this country to develop a comparable capability (and also to reduce the vulnerability of U.S. satellites), but the U.S. does not yet have an operational capability. An R&D program and testing of ASATs by the United States existed in 1963 (sic), but it was canceled by Secretary McNamara.

Both sides have antisubmarine warfare (ASW) capabilities. The United States is alleged to still have a lead in this category, but the U.S. program is designed primarily for warfare against Soviet tactical (i.e., nonstrategic) submarines, and in any event it is not believed that either side has a capability for attrition of SLBM submarines which is rapid enough to play a serious role in a nuclear war.[30]

Passive Defenses

When we turn to passive defenses, the asymmetries are even more dramatic. The Soviets have a massive civil defense program.[31] Since 1962, the Soviet civil defense program has been estimated to involve expenditures of $2 billion per year or more, and to engage over 100,000 full-time military personnel. In 1972, its status was upgraded by the appointment of its Chief, General of the Army A. T. Altunin, to the post of a Deputy Minister of Defense. The Soviet program includes the following elements:

(1) The protection of the Communist Party (the CPSU), the military-governmental infrastructure, "key workers," and people. The priorities here are clear. They are:
  (a) Protection of the leadership, corresponding to the U.S. concept of "continuity of government," including the top civilian leadership and military command, but also extending to all levels of civilian government and the Party, from what in U.S. terms would be federal down through state to local levels, and adding key industrial management personnel, for a total estimated to include at least 110,000 people;
  (b) The essential workforce, with blast and fallout shelters for 15 to 20 percent of the urban workers; and
  (c) The remainder of the population, which are to be evacuated from the cities and provided fallout protection.
(2) The protection of the sources of economic productivity, with programs for dispersal, duplication of key tooling, hardening, and continuity of production in wartime.
(3) The sustenance of the surviving population immediately following a nuclear attack and preparations for longer-term attack recovery (and in so doing, increasing the morale and purpose of the populace in crisis and in war).[32]

The United States, in contrast, has not had a serious civil defense program since the early 1960s. The Federal Emergency Management Agency (FEMA) mentioned in footnote 31 has a current budget of a little over $100 million, which at best amounts to five percent of the Soviet expenditure. FEMA's emphasis, however, is more on preparations for and assistance in times of disaster, both natural and man-made, than on protection in nuclear war. Early in 1978, when civil defense was still a Defense Department responsibility, Secretary Brown proposed a program to make plans for possible city evacuation, or "crisis relocation." It was a $2 billion program, but was to be spread over seven years—i.e., an expenditure of about $300 million per year. Asked at a press conference whether he backed a $2 billion program for civil defense, President Carter interpreted the question to mean $2 billion per year, or an effort comparable to that of the Soviets. He denied interest in any such plans.[33] In short, he cut the string, and Secretary Brown's trial balloon floated quietly away. It has not been seen since.

Passive defenses—hardening, proliferation, dispersion, concealment, mobility (enhancing dispersal and concealment)—apply to military forces also. Again, the asymmetries with the Soviet Union are great:

(1) Hardening—Both sides harden (that is, make resistant to blast and other nuclear effects) ICBM silos, nuclear storage sites, command-control facilities, and so on. However, the Soviet Union is believed to have far more numerous and harder targets in each of the above categories, especially in command-control (where civilian and military functions are sometimes collocated).

(2) Proliferation—Apart from earlier-noted differences in numbers of strategic systems, the Soviet conventional forces are far larger, with more tanks and other categories of weapons.[34]

(3) Dispersion—Soviet military targets are better dispersed (except for roughly comparable numbers of naval bases), partly because the Soviets are less prone than the United States to concentrate forces in a small number of large military bases (reflecting, among other things, the greater area of the Soviet Union and a lesser concern for isolating forces and thus decreasing the interface of weapons systems with the public).

(4) Concealment—Traditional Soviet secrecy versus the U.S. open

society creates gross asymmetries in the knowledge of military targets on each side.

(5) Mobility—Mobility in time of war increases both the dispersion and the concealment of forces. In time of crisis, which may also be a time of conventional war or the threat thereof, we must assume that Soviet forces will be moved forward toward or across their borders on many fronts (Europe, the Middle East, South Asia, and China)—i.e., "dispersed forward," reducing their targetability, and perhaps even putting some military targets off-limits. Whenever possible, the U.S. would want to encourage dissidence—not cohesion—with the Soviet Union, or even neutrality; with this in mind, would the United States want to target Soviet forces inside the PRC, the Middle East, or in Eastern Europe (let alone Western Europe)? U.S. forces, in contrast, may be unable to disperse in time of crisis. They almost certainly will not cross borders, and may indeed have to be massed at ports of embarkation, in order to be prepared to project power to overseas theaters.

The Roots of Asymmetry: Disparate Beliefs About Nuclear War[35]

The above-described asymmetries between the U.S. and Soviet strategic postures, and most especially between the strategic defensive measures of these two countries, did not evolve by chance. Rather, they reflect the dominant beliefs or attitudes in the two countries about nuclear weapons and nuclear war. While there can be and is a wide range of views on such an important and complex subject as nuclear warfare, the spectrum of views tends to be bimodal, or even bipolar. For simplicity, the two extremes will be presented—and in fact, the two extremes represent quite well the respective views of the United States and the Soviet Union.

The two poles may be described as follows. On the one hand, nuclear warheads are seen as weapons of total destruction, the use of which, once initiated, could not possibly be limited or controlled and would make survival of nuclear conflict impossible and the concepts of fighting and winning irrelevant. Since nuclear weapons exist and "the genie cannot be put back in the bottle,'' they must be used for deterrence only, not for warfighting. At the other end of the spectrum, it can be postulated that, while nuclear weapons are indeed revolutionary and horrifying, it is possible that they will be utilized, for reasons of accident or malign intent, and it is important to consider ways in which, if deterrence fails, nuclear war can be controlled, survived, fought, and won.

Patently, U.S. policy has been dominated by the first view, and as a consequence limited offensive forces are considered sufficient and defensive forces are viewed as both unnecessary and futile. For the past two decades, at least, Soviet doctrine and force planning appear to have been dominated by the second view: since capitalism and communism are antithetical and can never be reconciled, there is a constant risk that the imperialists will force warfare on the Soviet Union—by any means, including nuclear—and it is the unavoidable obligation of the Party, the leadership, and the people to do all in their power to survive and rebuff any such onslaught from the West.

The roots of these contrasting beliefs are undoubtedly numerous and complex. The writer will attempt to summarize those which he sees as dominant.

On the U.S. side:

(1) The United States is geopolitically an island power. Its long-term strategy must be to keep the enemy away from its shores, reaching out, if necessary, to destroy him on his own territory. In the 1930s and during World War II, there was widespread American acceptance of the doctrines of Douhet[36] and "victory through air-power,"[37] with its attendant abandonment of the feudal distinction between armed forces and civilian populations as proper objects of attack, and hence of threat.

(2) When the first A-bombs were used at the end of World War II, the federal government had an interest in maximizing the reported destruction of Hiroshima and Nagasaki. The legend was born that the A-bomb won the war rather than the more reasonable interpretation that it provided a beleaguered emperor with a face-saving basis for surrender.

(3) The nuclear revolution—with two successive hundred-fold multiplications in destructive power[38] plus invisible radiation that had long-term, insidious, and mysterious effects—struck terror in the

hearts of a people long-unused to being or feeling vulnerable. A guilt-ridden generation of scientists nurtured this terror and the beliefs it encouraged.

With respect to the Soviet Union:

(1) As a central land power, the Soviets always have others on their borders. Their strategy (and that of Imperial Russia) has always been one of expansion, pushing actual and potential enemies back and establishing buffers around the Great Russian heartland. Not always successful, they have several times been invaded and overrun. They have learned the necessity of being defense-minded, even while attempting to preempt their enemies offensively.

(2) The experience of invasion and dominance by enemies is logically consistent with acceptance of a universalist communist ideology that cannot permit giving up the objective of survival of the state.

(3) The imperative of expansion by force has taught the Russian/Soviet regimes that the use of power must be rational—not the nihilism of total destruction, not Douhetism, but the use of a doctrine of preemption with combined arms to prevail over enemies while leaving something to occupy and to afford a basis for coexistence, however temporizing, with antagonistic neighbors during nonviolent phases of diplomatic struggle.

Figure 1 reflects an attempt to portray the implications of these contrasting beliefs. The abscissa is simply the weight of a nuclear attack, measured in numbers of warheads, total megatonnage, or any other convenient unit. The ordinate is a notional measure of effective damage to the nation: 100 percent does not necessarily mean total destruction of all lives or physical assets, but elimination of a viable society and state. The upper curve represents the views of those who perceive nuclear war as apocalyptic, with even a relatively small attack rapidly approaching the point where society is destroyed and additional weapons represent overkill, asymptotically approaching truly total elimination of the nation.[39]

On the lower line, even moderate attacks create great damage, but only some very high level of attack creates the final rise of the line at the

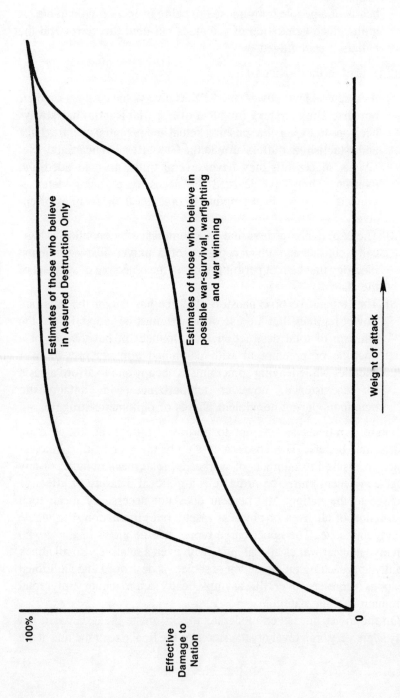

FIGURE 1. Effect of Beliefs on Estimates of Nuclear War Outcomes

right toward total destruction, which would result from the very high levels of radiation that at some point would prevent survival and recovery activities. It is the thesis of this analysis that the Soviets are determined to limit the weight of the attack to some point to the left of this "knee" in the lower curve, by means of (1) SALT limitations on numbers of weapons and (2) active defenses, including preemptive counterforce, that prevent as many as possible of the attacking weapons from arriving at their targets. Passive defenses are designed to push the lower line downward, reducing the effective damage resulting from any given level of arriving weapons.

This perspective is necessary for an understanding of the initial premises of this study. It is not intended to suggest that the Soviets do not fear nuclear war, nor that the Soviets "intend" a nuclear attack on the United States. Rather, it is believed that the Soviets are good Clausewitzians, preferring to win without fighting; that they have a much clearer concept than does the United States of the values for which they would fight rather than make concessions; and that they, rather than the U.S., truly design forces for deterrence, by making the use and effectiveness of these forces credible and by denying credibility to the U.S. deterrent.

What Deterrent Threats Can the United States Pose?

The writer has examined many 1980s scenarios in which a nuclear war starts with a Soviet counterforce attack—an attack on U.S. ICBMs, bombers on their bases, missile submarines in port, and command-control facilities for these forces. In every case, a U.S. Assured Destruction second strike (countervalue—against population and industry in large cities) appears to be deterred by the Soviet third-strike countervalue potential inherent in the Soviet Union's remaining withheld forces.

Even assuming that a future strategic arms limitation agreement (SALA) establishes realistically-equivalent Soviet and U.S. inventories of offensive and defensive strategic forces, several asymmetries appear to assure the Soviets an Assured Destruction weapons requirement which is lower than that of the United States.[40] The Soviet population is inherently more dispersed geographically than is the population of the U.S., and in addition the Soviets have the above-noted programs for dispersing and hardening their industry and for protecting their political leadership, key industrial workers, and general population. The question frequently asked, whether Soviet city-evacuation plans will work and can be sustained, appears to be irrelevant, because (1) Soviet emphasis is shifting toward shelter programs and away from evacuation and (2) the prospect of even partial success of their population and industry protection programs appears to enhance Soviet deterrence of a U.S. second strike. The achievability of Assured Destruction of the Soviet Union by U.S. forces is increasingly dubious; and surely will be more so if U.S. forces are further reduced in SALT.

Despite the shift (started by Secretary of Defense Schlesinger and continued under Secretary Rumsfeld and, after 1977, Secretary Brown) away from population targeting to threatening economic, political, and military targets, with emphasis on inhibiting or preventing Soviet economic and military recovery "more rapidly than the United States,"[41] the resulting "Assured Retaliation" appears to involve almost as great a threat as Assured Destruction to the Soviet population— if the population is not successfully defended. Old key questions remain: What levels of attack might cause the breakdown of civil order? Of the centrally planned economy? Of central authority over military forces? Subjectively, one strongly suspects that, while present weapon levels may be more than enough, 200 weapons (with how many warheads, and what "footprints," or coverage?) will not be. One also suspects that the value of repeated attacks will rise (see below).[42]

As implied above, it is generally assumed that the U.S. strategic forces would be among the first targets of a Soviet attack, either in a partially disarming first strike or as the first-priority targets in a larger preemptive strike. The question for American policy is whether a capability and doctrine for a U.S. attack on the Soviet forces would enhance deterrence and provide some damage limitation, should deterrence fail.

Crucial to the answer to this question will be whether the postulated SALT limits specify MIRV levels along with delivery vehicle numbers. Also critical will be the question of reduction or retention of vulnerable fixed basing, under agreements or unilaterally, by either side. If the Soviets retain their large proportion of fixed targets (ICBM silos), the United States may need (1) a capability to identify which Soviet silos have fired their missiles, as well as (2) warhead accuracy/yield combinations adequate for hard-target kill (a capability which could reside in weapons other than ICBMs—bombers may have it now; SLBMs could, eventually).[43] Enemy reload capabilities, after both cold-launch[44] and hot-launch, may dictate a U.S. counterattack on empty as well as full Soviet silos, but a U.S. capability may still be needed to identify the full and thus more time-urgent silo targets, since, as noted earlier, the Interim Agreement, the Vladivostok Accords, and the SALT II Treaty limit launchers only, not back-up missiles, which could be reloaded in silos (or fired from concealed surface launchers). At lower levels, it will become even more important to consider limiting numbers of weapons, not just launchers, with all the difficulty that this implies for verification.

Soviet doctrine calls for preemptive attack against other military and support targets as well as against strategic weapons systems. The author regards these Other Military Targets (OMT) as a sort of ''lower case'' counterforce, more general than the limited ''Counterforce'' case, above. He also believes that OMT constitute a potentially important target set for the United States, if they can be effectively located and attacked, in view of the high dependence of Soviet regime-maintenance on military power, as well as the increasing infeasibility and inherent immorality of attacks on population and civilian assets.

Particularly when strategic nuclear weapons are in limited supply, OMT targeting may be one of the more rational options available. A key question to be explored is: When heavy attacks are not feasible, would a credible deterrent be the threat to deprive the Soviets of (1) the capacity for internal control and peripheral defense, and (2) capabilities for projection of power to coerce distant nations in Western Europe? In East Asia? In North America? A special case relates to economic attacks designed primarily to impede economic recovery, since, if superior Soviet projection forces survived, they could be used to coerce assistance to Soviet recovery and to interdict assistance to U.S. recovery.[45] Whether there is a limited set of high-value military targets that would make such a threat credible with relatively small forces must be investigated (with use of ''all-source'' intelligence).

Finally, it is U.S. policy to maintain a capability for flexible response—i.e., the development and maintenance of limited nuclear options (LNOs) between all-out use of American strategic forces, on the one hand, and surrender, or accession to Soviet demands in time of crisis or conflict, on the other. Such limited options are intended to provide for responses appropriate or proportional to limited Soviet provocations or attacks; and to demonstrate U.S. will, conduct bargaining moves, control escalation, and negotiate for acceptable war termination "while something is left standing." The principal difference in the case of severely limited forces will be the question of capacity for carrying out such options without unduly impinging on the forces remaining for deterrence.

Prolonged War

Conventional scenarios of nuclear attack (Soviet counterforce attack—U.S. reply or concession; or Soviet all-out attack—U.S. all-out reply) may be quite unrealistic. Many levels and forms of nuclear war may be possible. Escalation *may* be uncontrollable, but it may also be the case that the incentives to control escalation will be very high on both sides.

It also appears likely that nuclear war will not occur out of the context of general war, including conventional land, air, and sea warfare. The available Soviet literature, including their own classified publications, discusses nuclear war in a global context, with theater operations occurring in a larger framework and nuclear exchanges seeming to take account of operations in one or more theaters. "Combined arms," to the Soviets, include nuclear as well as conventional weapons systems.[46]

In short, the conventional wisdom in the United States that a nuclear war will be short may well prove to be erroneous. Indeed, if one recognizes, as the Secretary of Defense now appears to, that the Soviets have a survival and warfighting doctrine for nuclear war, then the only possible U.S. doctrine to ensure a short war is surrender.

It is certainly reasonable to assume that any crisis critical enough to imply potential nuclear war would already involve conventional war. As this is written, the Soviets are in Afghanistan; numerous possibilities exist for expansion of the conflict into Iran and even, perhaps with Southern Yemeni proxies, into Saudi Arabia; and President Carter has warned the Soviets that any threat to Middle East oil supplies will be met by all means appropriate, including the use of force if necessary. Meanwhile, since the death of Tito Yugoslavia faces potential instability, with the possibility of Soviet intervention. Thus, any reasonably conceivable nuclear escalation in 1980 would occur in the context of spreading ground, and probably ocean, warfare. Early nuclear targets for the Soviets might even be U.S. carrier task forces in, say, the Arabian Sea. (American newspapers have published a picture of three U.S. aircraft carriers lined up, broadside, in perfect formation, with many escort vessels nearby—a potential and worthwhile single target for a large nuclear warhead or salvo of warheads.)[47]

A scenario with such diverse interests and theaters at stake might well involve limited nuclear attacks, even "probes." Resolution of all aspects of the war might well take many months, conceivably years, rather than the canonical hours, days, or weeks. Indeed, one potential strategy for the United States could be an attempt at limited political targeting. For example, targeting might be confined to the central Great Russian heartland, while avoiding any targets on the territory of potential Soviet enemies, internal as well as external. The intent to do this might be communicated to those peripheral nations and minority Soviet Socialist Republics in the USSR to encourage anti-Soviet actions, perhaps as a condition of continued U.S. forbearance.

In addition, the Soviets repeatedly refer to the importance of reserves:[48]

The outcome of a nuclear missile war is, in the Soviet view,[27]

> determined first of all by the reserve of nuclear weapons and means for its delivery to the targets as well as of other weapons and other material means which are produced and accumulated during peacetime, before the start of the war.

Hence, there is a need to estimate total possible expenditures and delineate "principles for creating stores of armament, combat equipment, and material resources, their echeloned location and storage."[28] The crucial tasks of military strategy . . . are[29]

> the determination of the composition of the armed forces for peacetime and especially for time of war; the making of a reserve of arms, military equipment, and primarily nuclear rocket weapons as the main means of war, as well as material reserves, deploying strategic groups and organizing the all-around security of the armed forces in times of war.

The concept of reserves of nuclear weapons and means of delivery refers to those forces remaining after the initial exchange or battle. It is that postexchange balance which is viewed as the primary measure of the correlation of nuclear forces.[30] In fact, an important scenario in Soviet strategy has the war continuing until one side exhausts its stock of nuclear weapons. If the other side still has a sufficient quantity (which appears to be measured at least in the hundreds), it then wins by default.

The richness of possible nuclear/nonnuclear scenarios, the possibility of prolonged conflict, and the importance of *secure, enduring* strategic reserves, plus C³I, should be kept in mind by the reader of the following sections.

The Parameters of "How Little is Enough?"

As indicated in the Introduction, at the time of writing (early 1980) the Carter Administration, continuing the trend of previous administrations, appears to have chosen, from the above menu of deterrence alternatives, the first option of Assured Destruction for the deterrence of major nuclear attack (as opposed to a counterforce or war-winning option), plus flexibility (or Limited Nuclear Options) for the deterrence of lesser threats. The Defense Department is conducting a continuing review of targeting options, following two major 1978 studies on Nuclear Targeting Policy and on Target Acquisition for the Secure Reserve Force (SRF). [Since this was written, Presidential Decision PD-59 was issued—and leaked in early August 1980—revising U.S. nuclear targeting doctrine to reflect these studies, emphasizing counterforce (including non-nuclear forces), leadership, and direct war-supporting industry targeting, *plus* a growing SRF to maintain an Assured Destruction capability to deter escalation to urban targeting. No major steps to implement this new doctrine have been taken.] Regardless of the ultimate effect of those studies and of SALT II on official U.S. doctrine [and regardless of what changes may be implemented by the new Reagan Administration], it is the purpose below to consider what doctrines may be feasible and sensible under hypothetical conditions of sharply decreased U.S. and Soviet strategic forces.

Actual numbers must, of course, be left to official channels, in view of the need to use classified data on the Soviet target systems (and those in other potential enemy countries) and to collect data on U.S. target systems in cases of important potential asymmetries. The U.S., or "Blue," target data base used by the Department of Defense is so much less complete and accurate than the "Red" (or Soviet) data base compiled by the Intelligence Community that the Department of Defense in 1978 and 1979 actually published U.S.-Soviet comparisons of strategic force capabilities on the basis of both sides' capabilities against the Red target set.[49] Because of widespread criticism[50] of this invalid procedure, the comparisons were dropped from the Department of Defense Annual Report for Fiscal Year 1981.

The next two sections will discuss military and politico-military factors that must be considered and will evaluate the sensitivity of U.S. security to variations in these factors, in the context of the possibility of decreases in the agreed levels of U.S. and Soviet strategic arms.

Military Parameters

Let us start with what we choose to call strictly military considerations. In each case, the sensitivity of U.S. security to the factor in question appears to rise as the level of strategic offensive forces declines. In other words, the risks are inversely related to the numbers.

Active Defenses

Consider first the role of the active defenses of the enemy: counterforce, air defenses, missile defense (ABM), antisubmarine warfare (ASW), and antisatellite (ASAT) weapons. The smaller the numbers of attack weapons, the more significant are active defenses.

Counterforce. The most effective active defense is that which destroys the enemy forces at the earliest possible stage—i.e., before they get off the ground. Declining forces may increase the value of preemption. A well-planned initial Soviet Counterforce attack—and planning the coordination of an attack with small forces will be simpler than doing so with large forces—may so decimate a small U.S. force as to be truly decisive, especially if Soviet conventional forces continue to be superior. Such a preemptive attack would include targeting of fixed ICBMs (if any remain in the force), SLBM bases (to eliminate SLBMs in port and to limit the endurance of SLBM submarines at sea), bomber bases (to destroy non-alert bombers and deny return to home bases of bombers that have been successfully flushed—although other recovery bases are presently planned for U.S. bombers), and C³I facilities (especially satellites—see below—and fixed ground facilities) to render surviving forces unusable.

Other Active Defenses. Active defenses may also be highly effective in the terminal phase (over the homeland) and, in the future, potentially in midcourse (between launch and terminal phase).[51] In particular, a Soviet technological breakthrough that surprises the United States might yield such an effective defense against small numbers of potential U.S. attackers that the United States would be effectively disarmed and completely at the mercy of Soviet diplomatic coercion. One cannot predict surprises, but the possibilities are manifold. They include: (1) rapid deployment of a new ABM system (a sudden "breakout" from the ABM Treaty), perhaps with a new warhead developed in clandestine testing under a Comprehensive Test Ban Treaty (the great exoatmospheric lethal range of "hard X-rays" against attacking missile warheads were a technological surprise from testing); (2) a breakthrough in antisubmarine warfare (ASW) permitting "trailing" of U.S. missile-launching submarines; (3) a more exotic breakthrough in high-energy lasers (HEL), directed particle beams, or other "death rays" that could bring down both ballistic reentry vehicles and aircraft; etc.

Even without surprises, active defenses are more effective against small than large attacking forces. One of the principal means of penetrating military defenses is by massing to overwhelm or "saturate" them. Bombers, for example, may be massed in one attack corridor to assure penetration. Defenses must be dispersed over all areas or approaches, since the offense has the "last move" (unless the defenses have very long range, so that the defense can regain the last move). Massing an attack increases its shock value. The shock is generally greater if 90 percent of a small target set is destroyed rather than, say, 10 or 20 percent of a larger set. Massing may maximize the economic impact on a region, and also the political impact, especially if it renders the region vulnerable to internal nationalism and/or external threats.

However, with small total forces, massing the attack limits the number of targets that can be threatened or attacked. For example, it may be more effective to attack a large portion of one or a few critical economic sectors rather than all industry in one region, but this may not be feasible if the sectors are dispersed through many defended regions.

Similarly, the Soviet leadership is likely to be too dispersed, sheltered, and concealed in crisis or wartime to be vulnerable to small forces.

Clearly, low bomber levels may not be achievable (or acceptable) in the absence of a limitation on air defenses. However, formulation and verification of such an essential limitation appear to present formidable difficulties, because: (1) air defense units are small and numerous; (2) strategic and tactical air defense systems are distinguishable, if at all, only by their location; and (3) radars and surface-to-air missile (SAM) systems may be mobile, making "suppression" difficult. It should also be noted that today's single Soviet ABM site, particularly with longer-range interceptors, could become significant at lower levels of permitted ballistic missiles.

One other category of active defenses is of extreme importance, at any level of forces. This is the anti-satellite (ASAT) capability, which is already a major problem at the current high level of strategic forces. As noted above, attack on U.S. satellites could be expected to be part of an initial, preemptive counterforce attack, in order to limit U.S. C³I capabilities at the outset. The Soviets have had an operational ASAT for several years. Currently, it does not use nuclear warheads and therefore does not count against the allowed numbers in the categories of offensive systems limited in SALT. The United States was testing an ASAT system in 1963 but abandoned the effort.[52] Only in the last couple of years has an ASAT R&D program been reinstituted, with the dual objective of threatening Soviet satellites and protecting U.S. satellites against the Soviet threat.

It is worth noting that the U.S. approach to an ASAT capability, in 1963 and today, has technological and operational advantages over that of the Soviets. (The loss of the U.S. lead was self-inflicted.) In the Soviet approach, a satellite is put in "quasicoorbit"[53] with the target satellite; the orbit of the killer satellite is then adjusted to intercept the target or to come close enough to use a short-range kill mechanism. The U.S. approach is one of "direct approach," growing out of ABM technology. An interceptor is launched, from the ground or from an aircraft, to increase coverage. The interceptor is then guided to or "homes" in on the target satellite. This approach has the advantages of (1) economizing on booster power and, more importantly, (2) accomplishing its mission more rapidly, with the possibility of intercepting killer satellites before they reach U.S. satellites. The latter can also be defended in other ways—with on-board weapons, or passively, by maneuver, hardening, redundancy, or standby replacements.[54]

There are also reports of Soviet progress in the development of high-energy lasers (HEL)[55] for "blinding satellites"—i.e., burning out their sensors and/or transmitters. If successful, this ASAT technique could also be extended to attack "geostationary" satellites at a 22,000-mile altitude. The latter are also vulnerable to "space mines" (nuclear armed satellites at the same altitude); these were prohibited by the Outer Space Treaty of 1967, but it is possible that a violation could not be detected by the United States, either at all or in time to respond before the space mines might be used. (A nuclear detonation could be effective in the vicinity of a U.S. geostationary satellite or at the "conjugate point," 180° away, on the other side of the world.)

Passive Defenses

As discussed earlier, in addition to active defenses, targets may be protected by passive defenses. Such defenses can increase the survivability of offensive forces, which is essential to both deterrence and warfighting capability and is of increasing importance as force levels decline.

Targets may have inherent, or natural, passive defenses, in that they are proliferated, dispersed, and hardened for social and economic reasons, as in the case of population and industry in general, or for tactical or administrative military reasons. Targets may also be deliberately (artificially) passively defended against nuclear attack, as in the case of civil defense programs, silo and command-control-facility hardening, etc. As in the case of active defenses, passive defenses may be particularly effective against limited attacks. By saving a portion of the assets attacked, they facilitate rescue, repair, or replacement of assets that have been hit.

However, it should also be noted that there are institutional and psychological limits to the implementation of passive defenses. Dispersal of plants takes a very long time, if reliance must be placed on dictation by the central authorities of the location of new facilities; it may run counter to managerial and labor interests; and it requires added resources for new infrastructure (transportation, power sources, housing, commercial facilities, etc.). Population relocation plans may be resisted by people who panic, doubt the threat, or follow orders improperly, etc., or by people in the "host areas" who feel unfairly burdened. The examples of such problems can be multiplied; in sum, they are what some analysts have in mind when they doubt the Soviet claims for the potential efficacy of their civil defense programs. In fact, in the event that these programs are used, the truth may well lie between the Soviet claims and the minimal effects predicted by the programs' strongest denigrators. What matters for deterrence, however, is not what U.S. critics believe but what the Soviet leaders believe. What matters in coercive Soviet diplomacy may turn out to be what the U.S. leaders believe the Soviet leaders believe.

There is also the possibility of surprise in passive defenses. This is an analogue of the possibilities of technological surprise (and rapid deployments) in active defenses, but different reasons apply. Civil and military passive defenses are characterized by low visibility, low obsolescence, and the possibility of rapid upgrading. Consider, for example, the extensive tunneling that surprised the French in Indochina and the South Koreans and Americans in Korea; the rapidity with which city evacuation might be implemented (especially, perhaps, in a tightly-controlled totalitarian society); the speed with which machinery might be protectively covered in factories; the extensiveness with which materials, parts, machinery, and end-products can be duplicated and stockpiled, slowly but unperceived; and the suddenness with which the deployments of military forces can be changed on the basis of contingency plans and under cover of military exercises. Surprise in passive, as in active, defenses will have much greater impact on downgrading the potential deterrent value of small forces than of large ones.

To increase survivability, three characteristics of passive defenses of strategic forces deserve special mention here:

Diversity. The United States presently relies on a "Triad" of forces (ICBMs, SLBMs, and bombers) for assurance against both surprise attack and technological surprise. There have been suggestions that, as the fixed ICBMs become vulnerable in the 1980s,[56] we should consider abandoning them (instead of, for example, putting them, or their successors, in a mobile or "multiple aim point" deployment mode).[57] There have been other suggestions that if the cruise missiles and/or their carriers become too vulnerable, we should abandon the airborne arm of the Triad and go entirely to sea, in which case, it is argued, the homeland would be exempt from collateral damage in counterforce attacks (violating the hostage theory of minimum deterrence).

As numbers decline and unit costs increase, it may be very tempting to rely on a "Dyad" or even a "Monad" in place of the current Triad. With small numbers, however, redundancy and hedges decline, and that may be precisely the time for prudence in the maintenance of the diversity of a Triad or even a "Multad."

Concealment. This includes system mobility, measured with respect to enemy intelligence-cycle leadtimes and weapon flight times (i.e., if it takes N hours for the enemy to detect and attack a weapon or C³I element, then that unit must move more often than once every N hours). Concealment also raises questions of SALT treaty formulation and verification.

Alert rates. This applies primarily to waterborne and airborne strategic platforms that are subject to close control and recall if launched on warning. Ships have historically "shown the flag" to demonstrate national will. In today's strategic arena, however, bombers are more effective than submarines, because submarines must stay concealed. These boats may be put to sea on warning, but their ballistic missiles (SLBMs), once launched, cannot be recalled, and their control is subject to tenuous communication links in wartime. Bombers need not hide or use other defensive measures until they reach enemy air defenses.[58] They are subject to close control and recall for six to eight hours, and even longer if they are refueled for loiter outside the enemy defenses. Thus, they provide time for reflection and negotiation that ballistic missiles do not.[59]

Other Force Capabilities

Other capabilities besides survivability are also important for the offensive forces. If the numbers of vehicles and warheads, and perhaps their sizes, are taken as given under SALT agreements, the capabilities of much-reduced forces become of increasing importance.

Reload/Recycle Capabilities. If silos can be reloaded with additional missiles, or extra missiles can be launched without silos, and bombers can return home (or to overseas "recovery points") and reload with fuel and bombs, then arms control agreements can be circumvented, especially under present formulations that limit only numbers of silos, submarine launch tubes, and bombers. This argues strongly (with large forces and even more so with small forces) for including the "Reload/ Recycle" parameter in future SALT negotiations and agreements. There is a trade-off involved here: reload/recycle for repeated attacks may have great value for the U.S.; but lack of limitation of this parameter clearly risks decisive Soviet superiority on such standby capability.

Survivability of reload/recycle capabilities is crucial and may not be symmetrical. The location and number of enemy reload or soft-launcher missiles will always be known better by the Soviets than by the United States. For bomber recycle, the Soviets have the advantage in defense attrition of U.S. bombers (since they have heavy air defenses and the U.S. does not), and in intelligence (since theirs is a closed society and American society is open). Moreover, as long as the United States has negligible air defenses, the Soviets will have, even with small bomber forces, a "free ride" for armed reconnaissance to seek out and destroy key surviving targets. Bomber attack planning may have to include protecting recycle capability, minimizing losses, minimizing enemy countermove capabilities, "ferrying" weapons (withholding some weapons during an attack for use in the next attack) versus prepositioning at recycle points, etc.

Accuracy. Increased accuracy permits high expected damage for given warhead yields and/or the use of lower-yield warheads, and thus lower collateral civilian damage, to minimize escalation risks. The limiting case is virtually perfectly accurate (zero-CEP) weapons used against point targets, which would make the substitution of conventional high explosives (HEs) for nuclear warheads adequate in almost every case. Do these then constitute strategic weapons not covered in SALAs (avoidance rather than evasion)? Will this mean a U.S. advantage? (How long will a technological lead last?)[60]

Reconnaissance. Reconnaissance acquires increasing importance as numbers decline:

(1) For verification, whether or not SALAs specify verification by national technical means;

(2) For monitoring avoidance; and

(3) For conserving resources: in the short run (intrawar), timely intelligence can focus attacks on undamaged high-value targets. Reconnaissance is improving, but not rapidly. No break-throughs, such as the satellite photography and other sensing capabilities developed in the 1960s, appear to be in the offing. Moreover, U.S. reconnaissance is threatened by the development of Soviet antisatellite systems.

Command, Control, Communications, and Intelligence (C³I). C³I also increases in importance as numbers decline. War, even more than most human activities, is almost always sloppy—battles are "ragged." C³I is more important for nuclear than for conventional forces, because accidents and mistakes are more serious and escalation is more threatening. Paradoxically, C³I is even more critical for smaller nuclear forces: escalation may not be quite as threatening, but accidents are, and conservation of nuclear resources to maintain deterrence, in crisis and intrawar, becomes more crucial.

Nonstrategic Use. As strategic force levels decline, it would appear that they must become increasingly dedicated to exclusive strategic use and unavailable for substrategic (theater—conventional or nuclear) use. Substrategic use of bombers has been important in the past and could be in the future. Conversely, proliferation of non-nuclear bombers would raise great, perhaps insurmountable, doubts about the observance of SALT limits: it may be well-nigh impossible to verify with national technical means the loading of nuclear weapons on medium- or long-range bombers. (On-site inspection, a conceivable future breakthrough for some purposes, would clearly need to be incredibly intrusive in this case, and hence is not really conceivable.)

Circumvention

A basic premise of SALT is that, by some agreed measures, both sides will have equal strategic forces. There are serious questions about whether this condition is met today, and hence whether U.S. calculations of force balance and potential nuclear war outcomes are based on valid numbers. Clearly, this problem becomes vastly more critical as permitted, or agreed, force levels may decline: the concealment of even small numbers of weapons could multiply small permitted forces, as against perhaps marginally increasing large forces. As in tax law, we may consider two means of "getting around the law": avoidance and evasion, or legal and illegal means.

Avoidance. Any forces not proscribed by a SALT agreement may, of course, legally be built. The SALT I Interim Agreement on Strategic Offensive Arms and the SALT II Treaty on the same subject both limit "launchers." Launchers are not carefully defined, but they refer to ICBM "silos," or in-ground, hardened ICBM launchers; SLBM launch "tubes" on submarines; and "heavy" bombers, currently defined as existing U.S. B-52s and Soviet Bisons and Bears. Nothing in the agreements limits the numbers of missiles or "medium" bombers.

First, with respect to the missiles: Both sides have always built "extra" missiles for purposes of evaluation testing, operational testing, and training. However, the United States has only a small inventory of undeployed Minuteman missiles and none in production, the Minuteman III line having been closed down two years ago. The Soviets, in contrast, are believed to have large numbers of missiles on hand, and have SS-17, SS-18, and SS-19 ICBMs in production. There is also an ambiguity in the SS-20 production; the missile is classed as of intermediate range (an IRBM), but can become an SS-16 ICBM with the addition of an SS-16 third stage (which the Soviets specified under SALT II they would not produce).[61]

The point is that, apart from the question of reload capabilities discussed above, extra missiles could be launched without silos. They could be launched from above-ground "soft launchers"—essentially gantries for the erection of the missiles, plus concrete pads under them and provision for venting of the exhaust gases from the rocket start-up. Such launchers could easily be concealed in the warehouses where the missiles are stored; the roofs could slide back or simply be penetrated by the missile on lift-off. They could also be floated in water and launched without any launcher, as has been extensively tested by both sides.[62] The United States simply does not know whether Soviet soft launchers exist, nor how many "standby" missiles there are at any moment.

Published estimates have ranged as high as four times the number of known silos.[63]

With regard to bombers, the United States has no medium bombers in production, whereas the Soviets have an estimated Backfire production rate of 30 per year. Note that the Backfire can reach the United States with refueling, and that B-52 missions against the Soviet Union would involve refueling as well; i.e., with respect to bombers, heavy versus medium is not the same as strategic versus nonstrategic.

In short, the possibilities of avoidance of SALT limitations are enormous. Moreover, the asymmetry between these possibilities in the closed Soviet and open U.S. societies is almost one of black and white. It is hardly conceivable in peacetime that the United States could conduct such activities clandestinely on any significant scale. Even if it were, the possibility that the Soviets would be worried would be small consolation for the awesome risk of such activities for the United States.

Evasion. It is also certainly not unimaginable that the Soviets would, at such time as it suited their purposes, evade or violate a SALT agreement. Such an action would raise several crucial questions. First, would it be detected by the United States before it had reached serious proportions (which could be quite soon at low levels of forces)? Even if one could have high confidence that such an action would be detected, the question of U.S. response carries many uncertainties. A countervailing evasion in the open society of the U.S. is as inconceivable as in the case of avoidance, as mentioned above. Furthermore, U.S. denunciation of the Soviet action, with an accompanying abrogation of the violated agreement, would be neither reassuring to the cause of peace nor reassuringly likely in view of the U.S. tendency to date to treat Soviet violations as "ambiguous" or simply minor.[64]

It is sometimes remarked that the U.S. is no worse off if the Soviets do something inimical to its interests in violation of an agreement than if they do the same thing in the absence of an agreement. In contradiction to this view, however, the fact must be noted that if taking a countervailing action requires abrogation of the agreement by the United States, that action is in itself a destabilizing move in international affairs of far greater conspicuousness and significance than a simple adoption of a new or increased defense program. Moreover, history suggests that such an action of abrogation is unlikely to take place.

Politico-Military Parameters

Military capabilities are necessary but not sufficient for the establishment and maintenance of effective strategic forces. The interplay of political factors with military capabilities must also (and always) be considered in negotiations about these forces and in planning deployment and employment doctrines for them.

Lesser Nuclear Powers

One must note immediately that the United States and the Soviet Union, while dominant, are not the only nuclear powers in the world. While the Chinese, French, and British nuclear forces today are of some concern to the Soviets, and the Chinese forces are perhaps also of some concern to the United States, at the present high bilateral levels of strategic forces these third-country forces do not enter importantly into the strategic equation. With sharp bilateral reductions by the two superpowers, however, these third countries could become "instant superpowers," because: (1) the superpower arsenals would be reduced toward their levels, and (2) the smaller nuclear powers might have an incentive that does not realistically exist today to start increasing their levels in direct competition with the present superpowers. In a world of three or more superpowers, deterrence and strategic calculations would be transformed. The instability normally associated with alliance diplomacy could return to a dominant role in international relations—carrying far greater risks than in the prenuclear world.

It is true that more of the present third nuclear powers are friendly to the United States than to the Soviet Union. Nevertheless, "plus, ca change, plus c'est la même chose" does not apply to alliances. On the contrary, history suggests that the one thing constant about alliances is that they change. The U.S. cannot count on the impossibility of a Sino-Soviet rapprochement. India, were it to build up its forces, *might* be neutral, but it might also be a case of "Irish neutrality"—in this case, "agin us."

Proliferation

There is the further vexing problem of nuclear proliferation. The disincentives for Nth countries to "go nuclear" in the past have often been underestimated. It took nineteen years for the fifth nation, the People's Republic of China (PRC), to join the "nuclear club," and another ten or more years for the next two to join (counting India and assuming Israel to be a member). Nevertheless, reversing "vertical proliferation" in the superpowers by cutting back their arsenals could decrease the disincentives to "horizontal proliferation" among nations. The economic and political price of entry at a competitive level could appear much less formidable, and the potential political and perhaps military utility of modest nuclear forces could appear much greater. It is probable that this phenomenon has already started, as a result of the loss of U.S. strategic superiority and also of apparent political will. The threatened, albeit halted, military pull-out from the Republic of Korea, abrogation of the treaty with the Republic of China (Taiwan), and perceived U.S. impotance in the Iran and Afghanistan situations may already presage much more rapid proliferation in the 1980s and 1990s (e.g., in Korea, Japan, Taiwan, Pakistan . . .).

The foreseeable Nth nuclear powers may appear more likely to be pro-U.S. or neutral. Furthermore, surely the Soviets, having been burned once (when they aided the PRC in nuclear development before the Sino-Soviet split in the late 1950s), are unlikely to provide other allies and satellites with nuclear aid, or even to permit them to "go nuclear." Again, however, as noted above, alliances—and policies— may change, and one cannot count on proliferation to be benign from the U.S. standpoint nor stabilizing from a global viewpoint.

Gray-Area Systems

A political-military problem that already complicates SALT is that of the "Gray-Area Systems." These are nuclear systems of greater range than the so-called "tactical" nuclear weapons designed for battlefield use; they are "theater weapons" of potential intersuperpower use. The name "Gray-Area Systems" is a SALT term of art; they cannot be defined "in black and white," except to the extent that they are systems not to date included in SALT, as distinguished from "Central Systems" that have been included. Examples are: intermediate and medium-range ballistic missiles (IR/MRBMs)—e.g., the Soviet SS-20, a mobile intermediate-range missile which can become an ICBM with the addition of the compatible SS-16 third stage or with off-loading of one or two of its three Reentry Vehicles (RVs); U.S. "forward-based" fighter bombers, deployed for the defense of Western Europe but capable of reaching the Soviet Union; "medium" bombers, notably the controversial Backfire, that with refueling (like heavy bombers) can be used intercontinentally; the recently planned NATO surface-launched cruise missiles and Pershing II ballistic missiles; and the Soviet Shaddock cruise missile, a 350-mile submarine-deployed weapon called an "anti-ship missile" by the Soviets but capable of use against many targets in the United States. As the Central Systems are cut back, Gray-Area Systems will look increasingly threatening, and the need to include them in an expanded SALT domain will become more urgent.

Tactical Nuclear Weapons

At some level, tactical nuclear weapons also become indistinguishable from strategic nuclear weapons, since platforms (e.g., ships) can always be found from which they can be launched against strategic targets. There are three implications of this fact:

(1) A constraining SALT agreement could be circumvented;
(2) Tactical nuclear weapons could constitute a "withheld force" after a strategic exchange that exhausted the SALT Central Systems and even Gray-Area Systems; and
(3) An attempt could be made to incorporate tactical weapons in a SALT-type agreement. (This would appear to be a terribly difficult, if not utopian, project.)

Lessened Deterrence of Conventional War

Declining numerical levels of nuclear weapons reduce their utility as an instrument of diplomatic coercion. This increases the influence of conventional forces, in which the Soviet Union is superior. Of special importance may be chemical warfare, for which the Soviets are prepared and the U.S. is not. Biological warfare possibilities could also become important.[65] We must ask, then, will SALT reductions ultimately "make the world safe for a conventional World War III"? Conventional weapons have become an order of magnitude more destructive since World War II, and America's NATO allies have no more desire to be destroyed by conventional than by nuclear weapons.

The above question takes on new meaning in an era in which the United States appears to be conceding strategic superiority to the Soviet Union. Ever since the U.S. demobilization following World War II (and despite the partial remobilization of the Korean War period) the United States and its allies have been willing to live with the existence of greater Soviet conventional forces because it was believed that the U.S. "nuclear umbrella" made major conventional warfare untenable. This assumption does not appear valid for the 1980s.

Can Deterrence be Maintained? Some Hypotheses

The above discussion is not encouraging. It suggests that while "small is beautiful" may apply with great appeal to strategic nuclear forces, there exist many complex problems and potential pitfalls if we are to seek such a goal.

Despite all these problems, minimum deterrence *may* work. Surely, no Soviet leadership will want to contemplate the horrors and uncertainties of nuclear war even if the threat is, say, hundreds instead of thousands of nuclear warheads. However, the issue is always: Who is most deterred in a crisis? It is not a question of either side deciding that "X million deaths are worth it," for whatever national interests are at stake in some future crisis. Rather, it is an issue of diplomatic coercion, of whose deterrence is greater, of who wins the battle of perceived capabilities and national will, of who blinks when "eyeball-to-eyeball."

The latent threat of nuclear coalition would also worry the United States. If the nuclear world indeed becomes multipolar, something reminiscent of Bismarck's nineteenth-century "cauchemar," or nightmare, of coalition may add to the deterrence and coercion of the United States. Furthermore, asymmetries in active and passive defense and in intelligence might create a credible perception of a greater threat with given limited forces against the United States than against the Soviet Union.

If low levels of strategic offensive forces are to be a U.S. negotiating objective, then the U.S. national security authorities (the Defense Department, the National Security Council, and the President) must analyze with great care the options that successful negotiation will leave open to them. From the above review of at least some of the relevant factors, the writer has derived some tentative hypotheses. They are not optimistic, but very little about potential nuclear conflict is.[66]

Hypothesis One: Assured Destruction is not today a credible option, and it will not be at lower levels of forces. Some of the reasons for the non-credibility of Assured Destruction were noted earlier in this paper. Carrying out the threat of Assured Destruction has never been a rational action; today, Soviet civil defense programs plus population distribution asymmetries between the Soviet Union and the U.S. mean that the Soviets could impose far greater "urban/industrial" punishment on the United States than vice versa—i.e., in a suicide pact, the U.S. would be "deader." Moreover, the SALT I Interim Agreement permitted the Soviets half-again as many ICBMs, with several times the U.S. throw-weight. The Soviets are MIRVing these missiles, and acquiring as great or greater accuracy than the United States. They were also permitted more SLBMs, which they are modernizing. Bombers were not controlled—the United States had more in 1972 (not counting the Soviet "medium bombers"), but U.S. numbers are declining while the Soviets are building the Backfire and developing a new bomber, and they have heavy air defenses while those of the U.S. are token only. By the early 1980s, the Soviets will have the capability to increase their advantage with a first strike on the U.S. Minuteman force, leaving their remaining forces greater than those of the U.S. and surely deterring the American deterrent.

Hypothesis Two: Economic threats, including that of enforcing slower Soviet than U.S. post-attack recovery, MAY be feasible, even with a significant decline in total forces. The United States does have a larger, more flexible, and probably more resilient economy. Its leadership and control mechanisms, being less rigid, may also be less fragile. The Soviet economy is far more autarkic, but U.S. dependence on imports *in extremis* is often exaggerated, as its World War II experience strongly suggested. On the other hand, Soviet preparations for "hardening" the economy (by protection of plants and workers, possible stockpiling, etc.) are apparently greater; as potential levels of damage decline, the hope of inducing economic breakdown may become chimeric. Finally, as noted earlier, recovery may be largely a function of relative surviving military power.

This brings us to the issue of counterforce targeting (again, per PD-59), in the writer's view a more proper use of armed forces than targeting civilians and their assets. This moral principle has particular force in the case of a population comprised of oppressed victims of the very totalitarian regime that would be attempting to coerce the United States if a crisis or casus belli existed.

Hypothesis Three: If strategic force levels are stringently curtailed, the special Counterforce case of strategic offensive weapons versus the enemy's strategic offensive weapons may be ruled out. With such limited forces, probably both sides, and surely the United States, will feel compelled to make their forces highly invulnerable. We are more concerned, therefore, with counterforce against other military targets (OMT), which leads us to the next hypothesis.

Hypothesis Four: There are important reasons for considering other military targets (OMT) for deterrence of the threats posed by Soviet forces under low SALT ceilings. These reasons have to do with the importance to the Soviet leadership of retaining power in any crisis or conflict. Regime maintenance must be a primary objective of the Soviet leadership. There are no electoral or other institutional arrangements for periodic or occasional changes in regime in the Soviet Union, even when the occasion is the death of the Chairman. At any given time, therefore, the regime must regard itself as permanent and must strive to maintain itself. The principal tools of its power are force, both military and paramilitary. A threat to destroy the means of retaining power, if feasible, may well be a deterrent to "adventurism" on the part of the Soviet regime in control at a given time. The argument gains force from the implication that signs of weakening power of the regime may stimulate both internal and peripheral resistance to that regime.

A Soviet counterthreat to U.S. military targets would not comparably threaten the U.S. leadership, which would not be primarily preoccupied with its own preservation of office. The United States does not have comparable internal nationalisms and dissidence. It is an "island" power without peripheral enemies. The President would, however, be deeply concerned with the potential collateral damage from such an attack, especially with respect to civilian casualties, as well as with the impact on the post-exchange U.S.-Soviet power balance. Of what use would it be to "win" a nuclear exchange, only to be at the mercy of Soviet naval and other conventional forces in the "recovery" period?

There is, therefore, a need for an in-depth examination of whether there exist a limited number of identifiable, targetable high-value Soviet targets, the loss of which could threaten regime maintenance. One can think of such possible targets—e.g., major concentrations of ground forces, major air and ground maintenance depots, major airfields, naval bases and shipyards, military (and political) command-control centers and facilities, and so on. How effectively the United States might target Soviet forces for internal control, peripheral defense, and projection of power (probably vulnerable in reverse order) could only be determined on the basis of full intelligence and a great deal of detailed analysis of the degree of hardness, dispersal, and concealment of such targets and of further dispersal practices in time of crisis.[67]

For analytical purposes, it would be necessary to create a comparable "Blue" target data base for the United States (on which we do not spend intelligence efforts comparable to those expended on "Red" for the Soviet Union) and to estimate what a comparable number of weapons could do to the United States, both directly and in collateral damage.

Pending such a detailed, two-sided study, the following further subsidiary hypotheses appear not unreasonable:

(1) There is an asymmetry in favor of the United States with respect to the vulnerability of the leadership and national stability to loss of military forces; and

(2) There are asymmetries in favor of the Soviets: (a) their military forces are larger and more dispersed, hardened, and concealed, at least in many categories (the United States has in recent years debated the closing of more than a hundred military bases, further concentrating, not dispersing, its target system); and (b) Soviet crisis dispersal plans may also be superior—while both sides' navies may have standing orders to put as many ships to sea as possible (U.S. ships are said to have the capability to remain at

sea longer, and in normal practice they spend less time in port),
one can imagine (perhaps unfairly) that the Soviet ground forces
have standing orders, perhaps rehearsed, to disperse on given
crisis signals, while U.S. "SOP" may be to "report to the parade
ground at high noon for further orders." This is undoubtedly an
exaggeration, but note that for the United States to "project"
significant conventional forces to overseas theaters it must mass
them at points of embarkation. (These are interesting questions,
and there are things that could be done on the U.S. side during a
period of force reductions through SALT X to improve crisis
dispersal.)

Hypothesis Five: The final category for deterrence defined at the
beginning of this paper, Limited Nuclear Options, will, with stringent
limitation of numbers, become increasingly unavailable for the deter-
rence of or response to limited attacks, the control of escalation (intra-
war deterrence), and war termination. This will be probable for two
reasons:

(1) All potential strategic attacks will be becoming more limited; and
(2) Limited numbers of weapons offer less scope for piecemeal
    nuclear attacks—probes and demonstrations of will—as we
    transit from a "weapon-rich" to a "weapon-austere" environ-
    ment. Premature, piecemeal use of weapons may appear to be
    dangerously self-disarming.

Hypothesis Six: Deterrence-only will become less and less feasible as
force levels decline, even if parity can be maintained with high confi-
dence. The United States is a status quo nation and its military philosophy is one of deterrence, not of warfighting. In strategic nuclear terms,
its philosophy and doctrine are ones of deterrence only. The Soviet
Union, in contrast, is a still-expansionist nation with a philosophy of
inducing change, by diplomacy where feasible, but by war as "an
extension of diplomacy" where necessary. Even at the strategic nuclear
level (and the Soviets do not make the sharp distinction that the United
States does between strategic nuclear and other levels of nuclear and
conventional war), the Soviets consider a warfighting capability, including defenses, essential—not only in order to preserve the mother-

land if the imperialists bring on a war but also to make their deterrent credible and to undermine the credibility of the U.S. deterrent.

* * * * *

The above hypotheses suggest that: (1) deep bilateral cuts may further one objective of arms control—i.e., limiting worldwide damage should deterrence fail; but (2) if they go too deep, such cuts will actually weaken the more important arms control objective of preventing nuclear and major conventional war, as well as undue concessions of national interests to avoid war. This implies the advisability of great caution and careful study of the implications of going too rapidly down this road (should the Soviets, for ingenuous or disingenuous reasons, agree).

Because the weakening of deterrence is a profound risk inherent in the present policy goals of the current and recent Administrations, we will list a number of measures that are essential for the amelioration of this national risk. These measures fall in two categories:

(1) Principles and policies for arms control negotiations, in or beyond SALT; and
(2) Unilateral measures that should be taken by the United States, whatever the pace of negotiated strategic force limitations.

SALT Implications

Massive reductions in strategic force levels would sharpen a number of concerns about SALT negotiations.

The Current Domain of SALT Is Far Too Narrow. There will be an increasing need to cover non-Central Systems in SALT. This means not only including some Gray-Area Systems but also expanding negotiations to merge with other, nonstrategic arms control forums, notably Mutual and Balanced Force Reductions (MBFR) in Europe. Furthermore, the further risks of a Comprehensive Test Ban Treaty to the already deteriorating credibility of the U.S. deterrent forces must be reassessed. Involvement of other nuclear powers in SALT becomes increasingly important, if still difficult and inimical to prospects for successful agreements. More parameters of strategic forces need to be brought under control, including, for example:[68] throwweight (or volume) rather than just numbers; weapons rather than just launchers; and defenses as well as offensive arms (limitations on air defenses and ASW operations, and reassurance with respect to adherence to the ABM Treaty).[69]

Verification Procedures Need to be Strengthened. Measures that will be needed are not likely to be verifiable entirely by national technical means. More cooperative and more intrusive means will have to be sought.

Dollar Savings are Likely to be Illusory. While economies are desirable, they should not supersede security as an objective. Lower agreed levels are likely in the long run to increase costs for: verification; intelligence; R&D hedges; standby nuclear weapons deployment capabilities; survivability (limited forces will require greater dispersion, mobility, concealment, alert levels, and reload/recycle capabilities—if these are not controlled—plus continued diversity, with attendant higher unit costs); and conventional forces.[70]

Increased Security may be Illusory. It will be necessary to find ways to measure the reduced deterrence that will come with reduced numbers. Is this compensated for by reduced damage potential? Ultimately, this may be a question of whether the likelihood of conventional war, including chemical warfare and perhaps even biological warfare, will be perceived as increasing, and, if so, how seriously.

Can We Get There from Here? Insofar as the likelihood of reaching an acceptable agreement on low force levels is a function of Soviet attitudes (which historically have emphasized the need for covering all targets), as well as those of third countries, we cannot know the answer to the question of feasibility. However, many problems remain to be answered unilaterally, as indicated in the next section.

Unilateral Implications

If SALT or other agreements on sharply reduced levels are reached, prudence will still require vigilant maintenance and implementation of a number of precautionary unilateral policies.

A Mixed Strategic Force will be Needed. The tradeoffs here are difficult. The traditional Triad arguments for assurance against both surprise attack and technological surprise appear to require greater force. At the same time, at low total levels a mixed force means very small force elements, and this means high unit cost and possibly low penetration confidence.

High Strategic Force Survivability will be Needed. Survivability means increased requirements for mobility, dispersion, concealment, reliability, and alert rates. All of these are costly, but alert rates are primarily a matter of operating costs and these are somewhat less separated and conspicuous, and therefore often more salable, than high unit procurement costs.

Highly Survivable, Enduring, and Effective Command, Control, Communications, and Intelligence will be Essential. Survivable, enduring, effective C³I will be needed for all elements of the strategic forces. If small forces are to accomplish their vital missions, all elements and units must be controllable with the highest confidence possible. We have noted that a future nuclear/conventional war is likely to be prolonged. C³I becomes increasingly essential to such a war. However, it is also most highly stressed by the high alert rates and intense, continuing tensions of prolonged nuclear/conventional war.[71]

U.S. Air Defenses Need to be Rebuilt. Air defenses have been reduced to token levels for "control of the sovereignty of U.S. airspace," on the argument that without ballistic missile defenses air defenses do not matter. If even modest numbers of enemy bombers are given a "free ride," however, a standoff in missile forces will not save us from coercion/defeat by the Soviets.

Civil Defense will be Needed. The United States cannot now or in the foreseeable future afford to ignore the growing U.S.-Soviet asymmetry in civil defense. Civil defense must be broadly defined to include a wide range of preparedness measures for the protection of population, industry (including the mobilization and recovery bases), and continuity of government (including protection of leadership, communications and information bases, and arrangements for post-attack federal-state-local cooperation). This broad interpretation is inherent in the new organization of the Federal Emergency Management Agency. However, the removal of responsibility for civil defense planning from the Department of Defense should not lead us to forget that civil preparedness is an integral part of the strategic military posture and not purely a civilian matter.

Continued Intensive R&D will be Needed. Since the potential destabilizing effects of Soviet technological surprises will be greater if the strategic forces are small, it will be essential to keep up with the state of the art in all potential strategic weapons, defenses, and C^{3}I, on order to prevent or limit surprise, and to have available standby technology to enable rapid deployment of responses to surprise.

Leadership Must Inspire Public Support. Inherent in a success or series of successes in reaching agreed reductions in SALT is a potential lulling effect. It will be necessary to make major efforts to ensure that there will be public support for the precautionary measures that such agreements will require.

New Doctrine will be Required. Finite deterrence becomes less and less credible as force levels become small. The potential of political and military attacks on the Soviet power base should be intensively investigated. *Soviet* values, as indicated by their doctrine and defense priorities, especially with respect to passive defenses, should be taken into account in targeting. The imbalance between the U.S. deterrence-only and Soviet warfighting, war-surviving, war-winning doctrines must be redressed.

The Mobilization Base must be Restored. In a "world made safe for conventional war" by progressive reductions in nuclear forces, the United States may find itself with the necessity of mobilization to offset Soviet conventional threats. Indeed, the increasing frequency and apparent intractability of international crises, and the increasing perception that a superpower conflict is likely to be prolonged, make the need for a viable mobilization base, and an increased level of mobilization, necessary for nuclear as well as conventional war.[72]

One of the most formidable U.S. deterrents to the Soviet Union would be its tremendous mobilization potential. (A strong case can be made in the wake of the Afghanistan invasion that the United States should mobilize today, but this argument is beyond the scope of this paper.) Today, the Soviet Union is in a state of mobilization comparable to that of the United States at the 1953 peak of the mobilization for the Korean war, at which time the U.S. was devoting 14 percent of its GNP to defense. Moreover, the Soviet effort has been at this level for fifteen years or more. U.S. defense expenditures are below five percent of GNP, the lowest level since before Korea, and its mobilization base is in disarray.[73] U.S. mobilization took three years in both World War II and the Korean war. Clearly, under these conditions, U.S. mobilization would take much too long to be effective in deterring or catching up with the Soviet Union. As a minimum, therefore, as the United States curtails its nuclear forces, unilaterally or by agreement, it must take concomitant steps to revitalize its mobilization base. This means a broad panoply of measures which can only be sketched here.

The industrial base should be prepared for rapid conversion, if and when needed, to the production of war matériel. This requires programs for the stockpiling of strategic materials and probably also key components and subassemblies; standby tooling for the production of bottleneck items (e.g., castings and forgings for aircraft, tanks, and infantry fighting vehicles); and production lines for key military items not in production today or with inadequate capacity for required wartime levels.

The military mobilization base would require the establishment of adequate war matériel reserves for the initial phases of a conventional conflict, as well as adequate trained manpower reserves (the Ready Reserves of the National Guard), and a standby registration and a standby draft. These steps would be in addition to the above-mentioned requirements for enduring C^3I capabilities and civil defense plans and preparations.

Standby legislative authority exists for most of the required actions. This legislation should be reviewed, and updated and supplemented as found necessary.

The essential ingredient, however, is national will. Both a mobilization base and mobilization itself require national leadership to mobilize the national will. External events can substitute for national leadership in this respect, but waiting for Pearl Harbors is too dangerous in the nuclear era.

Conclusion

It has become a cliché that larger U.S. and Soviet nuclear forces reduce security. Sharp and continuing reductions in these forces appear attractive, and ultimate reduction to zero nuclear weapons is an objective with wide appeal. Nevertheless, the above analysis drives one to important contrary conclusions. Some bilateral strategic force reductions may be feasible, *if they can be achieved equitably and verifiably;* but large reductions would lessen U.S. security, because they would involve the following intolerable risks:

(1) If both U.S. and Soviet strategic force levels are balanced, but very low, the balance can be more easily destabilized by:
  (a) Technological surprise;
  (b) Evasion (cheating);
  (c) Avoidance of limitations (i.e., the exploitation of loopholes by the legal expansion of forces in ways not covered by formal agreements);
  (d) Sudden breakout from the ABM Treaty or other subsequent defense limitations, and unforeseen increases in the effectiveness of passive defenses;
  (e) Buildup of the nuclear forces of present third countries (the PRC, France, Britain, India, Israel) and unanticipated alliance realignments; and
  (f) Further nuclear proliferation to new "Nth" countries.
(2) A shrinking U.S. strategic nuclear "umbrella" will:
  (a) Weaken alliance cohesion;
  (b) Increase the likelihood of conventional war;
  (c) Increase the likelihood of diplomatic coercion of the United States (i.e., appeasement); and
  (d) Impose a costly—both economically and politically burdensome—buildup of U.S. conventional forces.

The problem of finding numerical answers to the question "How little is enough?" has proved as intractable as answering the question of the 1960s, "How much is enough?" However, the analysis herein, and the conclusions noted immediately above, are believed to demonstrate that for a long time to come the answer will be neither zero nor a small number of strategic nuclear weapons. If the SALT process has acquired a "mad momentum" of its own, as is so often alleged about the building and improvement of armaments, then U.S. negotiators must be guided by the principles that:

   (1) U.S. military power, relative to that of the Soviet Union, must be restored and maintained, for the cohesion of U.S. alliances and the security of the nation and the Western world;

   (2) Large reductions in strategic forces must await the development of true verifiability, however intrusive; and

   (3) Utopia must wait.

NOTES

1. A "U.S. Program for General and Complete Disarmament in a Peaceful World" was submitted to the United Nations on November 25, 1961.

2. This is loose phraseology. The adjective "strategic" refers to "Central Systems" involving nuclear warfare between the United States and the Soviet Union and implying involvement of the homelands of the two superpowers. As we shall see below, the term "strategic" has defied precise definition. "Strategic" and "Central Systems" mean what the SALT negotiators say they mean.

3. "Basic Principles of Mutual Relations Between the United States of America and the Union of Soviet Socialist Republics," signed in Moscow on May 29, 1972 (following the May 26 signing of the ABM Treaty and the Interim Agreement on Offensive Arms).

4. Rowland Evans and Robert Novak, "Nuclear 'Blockbuster'," *The Washington Post,* January 27, 1977, p. A-24. Also, Edward Walsh and George C. Wilson, "Carter to Get Study on A-Deterrence," *The Washington Post,* January 28, 1977, p. A-3. Evans and Novak referred to a meeting on January 12, 1977 between Carter, Defense Secretary-Designate Harold Brown, and General George Brown, Chairman of the Joint Chiefs of Staff.

5. Harold Brown, *Department of Defense Annual Report, Fiscal Year 1979.*

6. See his Ann Arbor speech of June 16, 1962, in Robert S. McNamara, *The Essence of Security* (New York: Harper & Row, 1969).

7. See Alain Enthoven and K. Wayne Smith, *How Much is Enough? Shaping the Defense Program, 1961–1969* (New York: Harper & Row, 1971).

8. McNamara's Assured Destruction criteria changed each year from 1964 to 1967. They ranged from 20 to 33 percent destruction of population and from 50 to 67 percent of industry, and in 1968 he simply called for a capability to inflict "an unacceptable degree of damage" and "to destroy the attacker as a viable 20th Century nation. . . ." See Department of Defense Appropriations, Subcommittee on the Department of Defense of the Committee on Appropriations, U.S. Senate, 88th Congress, 1st and 2nd Sessions on H.R. 7179 and 10939, respectively, pages 40 and 33, respectively, and 89th Congress, 2nd Session, Part 1, p. 44; also Statements of Secretary of Defense Robert S. McNamara before Joint Sessions of the Senate Armed Services Committee and the Senate Subcommittee on Department of Defense Appropriations, for Fiscal Years 1966, 1968, and 1969, pp. 45, 39, and 47, respectively.

9. The author has described and analyzed these changes in a series of books entitled *Arms, Men, and Military Budgets: Issues For Fiscal Year 1977, 1978, 1979, and 1981*. The volumes for *FY1977* and *FY1978* were edited by Francis P. Hoeber and William Schneider, Jr. (New York: Crane, Russak and Co., 1976 and 1977, respectively). The volume for *FY1979* was co-authored by Francis P. Hoeber, David B. Kassing, and William Schneider, Jr. (New York: Crane, Russak and Co., 1978). The volume for *FY1981* was co-authored by Francis P. Hoeber, William Schneider, Jr., Norman Polmar, and Ray Bessett (New Brunswick: Transaction Press, 1980). See also James R. Schlesinger, *Department of Defense Annual Report, Fiscal Year 1976 and 1977T*, and Donald H. Rumsfeld, *Department of Defense Annual Report, Fiscal Year 1977*, pp. 46–49.

10. Melvin R. Laird, *Department of Defense Annual Report, Fiscal Year 1973*, p. 2.

11. Briefing of the Overseas Writers Association, January 10, 1974.

12. James R. Schlesinger, *Department of Defense Annual Report, Fiscal Year 1975*.

13. Donald H. Rumsfeld, *Department of Defense Annual Report, Fiscal Year 1977*, p. 46.

14. Donald H. Rumsfeld, *Department of Defense Annual Report, Fiscal Year 1978*, pp. 68–69.

15. Harold Brown, *Department of Defense Annual Report, Fiscal Year 1979*, p. 55.

16. Harold Brown, *Department of Defense Annual Report, Fiscal Year 1981*, p. 68.

17. *Ibid.*, p. 65.

18. There is no universally accepted definition of a "nuclear power." Certainly Britain, France, and the People's Republic of China are counted. We

assume Israel is. Many apply the term to India because it has exploded a "nuclear device."

19. Note that these are at once cosmic and severely constrained questions. The writer has expressed elsewhere considerable skepticism about the prospects of SALT and concern about the imminence of Soviet strategic superiority and the diplomatic uses of that superiority. See Francis P. Hoeber, "SALT I: The Morning After," Rand P-4867 (Santa Monica: The Rand Corporation, July 1972); Amoretta M. Hoeber and Francis P. Hoeber, "SALT: Options for the New Administration," *Armed Forces Journal*, January 1977; Francis P. Hoeber in the *Arms, Men, and Military Budgets* series; and Francis P. Hoeber, "Defense Expenditures and SALT II," *National Security Record*, October 1979.

20. "Strategic nuclear delivery vehicles" refers to the "Central Systems" covered in SALT: ICBMs (intercontinental ballistic missiles), SLBMs (submarined-launched ballistic missiles), and heavy (long-range) bombers—at present defined as B-52s and Soviet Bisons and Bears. Note, however, that for missiles the item controlled is really launchers—ICBM silos and SLBM "launch tubes"—not vehicles per se.

21. The Afghanistan invasion was the announced reason. There had been, however, considerable controversy as to whether the Administration could muster the 67 votes required for approval of ratification, and one can only speculate as to whether the Treaty would have been brought before the Senate during this election year and, if so, whether it would have passed. In any event, President Carter has announced that the United States will continue to abide by the provisions of the Treaty, as long as the Soviets do. See *The Washington Star*, January 5, 1980, p. A-4 and January 6, 1980, p. A-8.

22. Medium bombers include: on the Soviet side, about 300 aging Badgers and over 100 modern, supersonic Backfires, with the number estimated to reach 375 to 400 during the period of the Treaty; on the U.S. side, 75 FB-111s with none currently in production.

23. For a more comprehensive treatment of the SALT II Treaty and its implications than can be given here, see Francis P. Hoeber, "The SALT II Treaty and the Security of the United States"; William Schneider, Jr., "Analysis of the Protocol, Joint Statement of Principles, and the Soviet Backfire Statement"; Robert L. Pfaltzgraff, Jr., "Verification and the SALT II Treaty"; and Colin S. Gray, "SALT II and the NATO Alliance," all in *International Security Review*, Volume IV, No. II, Summer 1979.

24. *Aviation Week and Space Technology*, April 3, 1978, p. 3. The warhead yield is also larger, contributing to the effectiveness against hard targets. Last year, the estimate of the yield of the Soviet SS-18 was downgraded from 1.2 megatons to .6 megatons; see *The Washington Post*, May 31, 1979, p. 3.

25. Only the 550 Minuteman IIIs are MIRVed, with only 3 Mark 12 warheads of 170 kilotons (KT) each, or over 300 KT in the Mark 12A (being retrofitted to 300 of the missiles); these could eliminate at most only about 50 percent of the Soviet ICBM force if the United States were to consider a counterforce first strike.

26. Harold Brown, *Department of Defense Annual Report, Fiscal Year 1981*, p. 85.

27. A proposal was made by the Senate Armed Service Committee in June 1980 (see *The Washington Post*, June 14, 1980, p. 4) to use 100 3-warhead MIRVed Minuteman IIIs to replace 100 single warhead Minuteman IIs, thus increasing the total number of warheads by 200. Minuteman III warheads are smaller but more accurate. Note (1) that fewer missiles would remain for continued operational testing and training and (2) that we would then have 650 MIRVed ICBMs, still well below the SALT II limit of 820, which the Soviets will probably reach by 1982. Whether and when we might exceed the over-all MIRV limit of 1200 will depend on policy decisions with respect to the deployment of Trident submarines and the retirement of older boats.

28. The ZSU-23-4 (with four 23-mm. barrels) and the ZSU-57-2 (with two 57-mm. barrels).

29. James R. Schlesinger, *Department of Defense Annual Report, Fiscal Year 1975*, p. 66.

30. This belief is based on the common assumption that any nuclear war will be a short one. We will come later to the question of whether this is a valid assumption, but can defer this complexity in the present context, noting only that if a war is prolonged, even slow attrition of missile-carrying submarines may be significant.

31. The term "civil defense" has a rather narrow connotation in the U.S., where it generally covers the protection of the civilian population only. As will be seen, to the Soviets it has a broader meaning, including the protection of leadership and industry and preparations for wartime economic functions. We will use the term in its broader sense here, since the 1979 creation of the Federal Emergency Management Agency (FEMA) brought together the previously separate population defense responsibilities of the Defense Civil Preparedness Agency (DCPA) and the other preparedness functions of the Federal Preparedness Agency (FPA).

32. See (1) *Soviet Civil Defense*, unclassified report, Director of Central Intelligence, July 1978; (2) "An Analysis of Civil Defense in Nuclear War," U.S. Arms Control and Disarmament Agency, NI 78-1003, December 1978; (3) "The 'Mine Shaft Gap' Revisited: Soviet Civil Defense and U.S. Deterrence," U.S. Representative Les Aspin, December 1978; (4) an evaluation of the three items just listed, "Toward a More Balanced View of Soviet Civil

Defense: A Critique of U.S. Assessments," Advanced International Studies Institute, for the Defense Nuclear Agency, June 9, 1979; (5) Leon Goure, *War Survival in Soviet Strategy, USSR Civil Defense* (Miami: Center for Advanced International Studies, University of Miami, 1976); Chuikikof, *Civil Defense* [Grazhdanaskaya Oborona] (Moscow: 1969), translated and edited by Oak Ridge National, April 1971; and (7) T.K. Jones, Testimony to the House Armed Services Committee, Subcommittee on Investigations, Civil Defense Panel, February 26, 1976.

33. President Carter at a news conference on November 30, 1978, as reported in U.S. Air Force *Selected Statements,* January 1, 1979, p. 56.

34. The Soviets have a three-to-one edge in manpower, and a four-to-one advantage in tanks. See John M. Collins, *American and Soviet Military Trends Since the Cuban Missile Crisis* (Washington, D.C.: Center for Strategic and International Studies, Georgetown University, 1978), pp. 174–94.

35. The concepts in this section are discussed more fully in a recent article by Richard B. Foster and Francis P. Hoeber, "Ideology and Economic Analysis: The Case of Soviet Civil Defense," *Comparative Strategy,* Vol. 1, No. 4, 1979.

36. Giulio Douhet, *The Command of the Air,* ed. by Dino Ferrari (New York: Arno Press, 1972, Reprint Edition—the Second Edition was first published, in Italian, in 1927).

37. Alexander P. Seversky, *Victory Through Air Power* (New York: Simon and Schuster, 1942).

38. Yields increased a thousand-fold each time—from tons of TNT to kilotons and then megatons of "TNT equivalent"—but destructive power follows the "two-thirds power law," i.e.:

$$D = Y^{2/3}$$

where D = destructive power and
Y = yield, in kilotons or megatons.

Thus, for the transitions from tons (high-explosive bombs) to kilotons (A bombs—fission) to megatons (H bombs—fusion), the increases in destructive power cited in the text were derived as follows:

$(1,000)^{2/3} = 100$ and $(1,000,000)^{2/3} = 10,000 = (100)(100)$.

39. For example, Herbert York said in *Scientific American,* August 1969, p. 10, "One hydrogen bomb on one city of one's own country would be recognized in advance as a catastrophic blunder; ten bombs on ten cities would be a disaster beyond history; and one hundred bombs on one hundred cities are

unthinkable." McGeorge Bundy quoted the above with approval in "To Cap the Volcano," *Foreign Affairs,* October 1969.

40. Whether the Soviets have an Assured Destruction objective is not at issue here. It is U.S. perceptions of Soviet capabilities that will influence U.S. behavior.

41. Donald H. Rumsfeld, *Department of Defense Annual Report, Fiscal Year 1978,* p. 68.

42. See Hoeber and Schneider, eds., *Arms, Men, and Military Budgets: Fiscal Year 1978* for a more extended discussion of why both Assured Destruction and Assured Retaliation have become increasingly infeasible for the United States.

43. A Comprehensive Test Ban (CTB) Treaty, as is now under negotiation, would prevent the achievement of better yield-to-weight ratios by the United States, as well as adequate testing for high-confidence maintenance of warhead inventories. It would be subject to undetected evasion by the Soviets with low-yield explosions "decoupled" from seismic shock by the use of large underground cavities. If the Soviets could thus continue testing when the U.S. could not, they might in time also make substantial advances that could result in a decisive technological surprise for the United States. The United States is too open a society to do likewise. The fate of CTB probably rests on that of SALT II.

44. "Cold-launch" means that the first rocket motors are not ignited while the missile is in its silo or launch tube. The missile is "popped up" by a gas generator, and then the rockets are ignited. Since hot gases damage a silo, cold launch permits "rapid reload." (It also permits greater efficiency in terms of the maximum throwweight achievable from a silo of given size.) The Soviets have cold-launched SS-17 and SS-18 ICBMs. The U.S. cold-launches its SLBMs.

45. Note that the start and rate of economic recovery after World War II in Europe (on both sides of the Iron Curtain) and Japan was virtually dictated by U.S. and Soviet policies, backed by the latent power of these countries to support or inhibit that recovery.

46. See Joseph D. Douglass Jr. and Amoretta M. Hoeber, *Soviet Strategy for Nuclear War* (Stanford: Hoover Institution Press, 1979).

47. *The Washington Post,* February 7, 1980, p. 1.

48. Joseph D. Douglass, Jr. and Amoretta M. Hoeber, op. cit. Their footnotes are as follows:

    27. Col. A. Gurov, "Economics and War," *Voyennaya mysl'* 1965, no. 7 (July), FDD 962, trans. 5/25/66, p. 7.

    28. Marshal of the Soviet Union V. D. Sokolovskiy and Maj. Gen. M. Cherednichenko, "Military Strategy and Its Problems," *Voyennaya mysl'* 1968, no. 10 (October), FPD 0084/69, trans. 8/29/69, p. 37.

29. V. D. Sokolowskiy and Gen. Maj. Cherednichenko, "On Contemporary Military Strategy," in *The Nuclear Revolution in Soviet Military Affairs,* trans. and ed. by William R. Kintner and Harriet Fast Scott (Norman, Okla.: University of Oklahoma Press, 1968), p. 271.

30. Maj. Gen. I. I. Anureyev, "Determining the Correlation of Forces in Terms of Nuclear Weapons," *Voyennaya mysl'* 1967, no. 6 (June), FPD 0112/68, trans. 7/11/68, p. 40.

49. Lt. Gen. Kelley Burke, "Quantifying the Strategic Balance," A Paper Presented at the Second Dyadic Seminar on Foreign Policy, Monterey, California, December 7–9, 1979.

50. See, for example: "An Evaluation of U.S. and Soviet Strategic Capability Through the Mid-1980s: A Comparative Analysis," The Committee on the Present Danger, September 29, 1978; Francis P. Hoeber, in *Arms, Men, and Military Budgets: Issues for the Fiscal Year 1981,* Chapter 2; and "DoD Used Wrong Targets Analyzing Outcome of U.S./U.S.S.R. Nuclear Exchange," *Armed Forces Journal,* April 1979, p. 11.

51. In the case of cruise missiles, the high value of a cruise missile carrier before it launches its missiles will make it a very tempting target outside of the Soviet (terminal) defended airspace. Many means of such attack may be feasible, utilizing long-range or forward-based radars (at-sea or on satellites) and long-range interceptors, sea-based SAMs, or even ballistic missiles.

52. See *Defense/Space Daily,* November 18, 1977, p. 20, and Robert C. Aldridge, "Who will shoot first in space?" *The Nation,* March 25, 1978, p. 334.

53. "Quasicoorbit" means an orbit close enough to that of the target satellite to permit maneuver to intercept.

54. For a fuller discussion, see the author's Chapter Four, "Active Defenses: U.S. Strategic Options in the 1980s," in William R. Van Cleave and W. Scott Thompson, eds., *Strategic Options for the Early Eighties: What Can be Done?* (New York: National Strategy Information Center, 1979).

55. See *Aviation Week and Space Technology,* June 16, 1980, p. 58.

56. In his *Department of Defense Annual Report, Fiscal Year 1981,* p. 85, Secretary Brown noted: "Although the Soviets have only just begun to deploy a version of the SS-18 IRBM with 10 MIRVs, within a year or two we can expect them to obtain the necessary combination of ICBM numbers, reliability, accuracy, and warhead yield to put most of our Minutemen and Titan silos at risk from an attack with a relatively small proportion of their ICBM forces. For planning purposes, therefore, we must assume that the ICBM leg of our Triad could be destroyed within a very short time as one result of a Soviet surprise attack."

57. There have been many such proposals. The series of complex basing

modes suggested for the MX—from tunnels through racetracks to the current linear road proposal—have been complicated primarily by the perceived necessity to make their numbers verifiable by the Soviets within the U.S. perception of what is permitted under the SALT II Treaty (even though the present schedules do not call for the deployment of the MX until after the expiration of the Treaty at the end of 1985). See Jeffrey G. Barlow, "Insuring Survivability: Basing the MX Missile," *The Heritage Foundation Backgrounder*, No. 120, May 27, 1980, and William Schneider, Jr., "Survivable ICBMs," *Strategic Review*, Vol. VI, No. 4, Fall 1978. For a concise summary of MX basing proposals, see *Aerospace Daily*, June 23, 1980, p. 294. Schemes for earlier reduction in the vulnerability of Minuteman by the digging of more silos in the present Minuteman fields among which the Minuteman missiles could be moved in a "shell game" and into which the MX could eventually be deployed are discussed in *Strategic Options for the Early Eighties*, Chapter Six. There are also interesting, and not necessarily highly costly, possibilities of defending the silos containing missiles with new types of ABM systems. See Francis P. Hoeber in *Strategic Options for the Early Eighties*, cited above.

58. This may be subject to change in the future. With adequate satellite surveillance, bombers could be attacked in midcourse with large ballistic missile warheads or other means. Evasive action by the bombers—changing course—would in turn require impressive capabilities for surveillance and assessment of enemy launches, elaborate and survivable communications to the bombers, and penalties in bomber fuel consumption and tanker support requirements.

59. See the author's *Slow to Take Offense: Bombers, Cruise Missiles, and Prudent Deterrence* (Washington, D.C.: Center for Strategic and International Studies, Georgetown University, 1977; second edition, 1980).

60. It was reported two years ago that Soviet tests had shown SS-18 and SS-19 accuracies approaching 0.1 nautical miles (600 feet), better than the reported Minuteman III accuracy and equal to the accuracy Minuteman III may achieve in the early 1980s. See *Aviation Week and Space Technology*, April 3, 1978.

61. See the "Common Understanding" associated with Article IV, paragraph 8 of the SALT II Treaty.

62. Paul A. Chadwell, "Floating-launched Ballistic Missiles," *National Defense*, April 1980, pp. 24–27.

63. Maj. Gen. George Keegan, in *Aviation Week and Space Technology*, March 28, 1977, p. 46. See also John Erickson, "The Soviet Military System: Doctrine, Technology and 'Style'," unpublished manuscript, p. 21.

64. Melvin Laird, "Arms Control: The Russians are Cheating!" *Reader's Digest*, December 1977, p. 97; Senator Gordon Humphrey, "Analysis and

Compliance Enforcement in SALT Verification,'' *International Security Review,* Vol. 5, No. 1, Spring 1980, p. 1.

65. Note the recent evidence of Soviet violation of the Treaty ban on production of biological agents revealed by the explosion of a factory in Sverdlovsk that spread pulmonary anthrax. See *The Washington Post,* June 29, 1980, p. 2.

66. It was noted earlier that nuclear weapons appear to have deterred major war (nuclear or conventional) for over thirty years. This may be true, but it is not knowable. We know there has been no World War III, but we cannot know that this is because of nuclear weapons—i.e., that without those weapons there would have been a major war. However, if nuclear deterrence was in fact the reason for peace, the question of major importance is now: Can this deterrence continue in the future?

67. One of the least improbable crises of the sort that might at some time be sufficiently serious to require a nuclear threat and/or attack would be a war in Europe. In such a scenario, many of the Soviet target systems of interest might well be dispersed forward into Europe, where they would be difficult to attack and would involve collateral damage to American allies and to potential U.S. allies in Eastern Europe. Another scenario might be in the Middle East. Would the United States want to explode the first nuclear warhead on an Islamic people?

68. The potential usefulness of the throwweight limitation concept is discussed at length in Amoretta M. Hoeber and Francis P. Hoeber, ''SALT: Options for the New Administration,'' op. cit.

69. The United States has proposed limitations on civil defense, and a Task Force has been set up for U.S.-Soviet discussions of the question. Civil defense is not included above simply because the author cannot at present conceive of ways for effective, verifiable limitations in this area. At time of writing, no progress has been reported by the Task Force.

70. These points were made by the author in 1963. See Francis P. Hoeber, ''The Economic Impacts of Disarmament,'' *Orbis,* Vol. VII, No. 3, Fall 1963.

71. See Paul Bracken, ''Command and Control for a Long War,'' *Air Force Magazine,* April 1980, p. 50.

72. See Paul Bracken, ''Mobilization for the Nuclear Age,'' *International Security,* Vol. 3, No. 3, Winter 1978/79, p. 74.

73. See John J. Fialka, ''The Grim Lessons of Nifty Nugget,'' *Army,* April 1980; and ''Why the U.S. Can't Rearm Fast,'' *Business Week,* February 4, 1980, p. 80.

National Strategy Information Center, Inc.

PUBLICATIONS

Frank N. Trager, Editor
Dorothy E. Nicolosi, Associate Editor
Joyce E. Larson, Managing Editor

STRATEGY PAPERS

How Little is Enough? SALT and Security in the Long Run by Francis P. Hoeber, January 1981

Raw Material Supply in a Multipolar World by Yuan-li Wu, October 1973. Revised edition, October 1979

India: Emergent Power? by Stephen P. Cohen and Richard L. Park, June 1978

The Kremlin and Labor: A Study in National Security Policy by Roy Godson, November 1977

The Evolution of Soviet Security Strategy 1965–1975 by Avigdor Haselkorn, November 1977

The Geopolitics of the Nuclear Era by Colin S. Gray, September 1977

The Sino-Soviet Confrontation: Implications for the Future by Harold C. Hinton, September 1976 (Out of print)

Food, Foreign Policy, and Raw Materials Cartels by William Schneider, Jr., February 1976

Strategic Weapons: An Introduction by Norman Polmar, October 1975 (Out of print)

Soviet Sources of Military Doctrine and Strategy by William F. Scott, July 1975

Detente: Promises and Pitfalls by Gerald L. Steibel, March 1975 (Out of print)

Oil, Politics and Sea Power: The Indian Ocean Vortex by Ian W.A.C. Adie, December 1974 (Out of print)

The Soviet Presence in Latin America by James D. Theberge, June 1974

The Horn of Africa by J. Bowyer Bell, Jr., December 1973

Research and Development and the Prospects for International Security by Frederick Seitz and Rodney W. Nichols, December 1973

The People's Liberation Army: Communist China's Armed Forces by Angus M. Fraser, August 1973 (Out of print)

Nuclear Weapons and the Atlantic Alliance by Wynfred Joshua, May 1973 (Out of print)

How to Think About Arms Control and Disarmament by James E. Dougherty, May 1973 (Out of print)

The Military Indoctrination of Soviet Youth by Leon Goure, January 1973 (Out of print)

The Asian Alliance: Japan and United States Policy by Franz Michael and Gaston J. Sigur, October 1972 (Out of print)

Iran, the Arabian Peninsula, and the Indian Ocean by R. M. Burrell and Alvin J. Cottrell, September 1972 (Out of print)

Soviet Naval Power: Challenge for the 1970s by Norman Polmar, April 1972. Revised edition, September 1974 (Out of print)

How Can We Negotiate with the Communists? by Gerald L. Steibel, March 1972 (Out of print)

Soviet Political Warfare Techniques, Espionage and Propaganda in the 1970s by Lyman B. Kirkpatrick, Jr., and Howland H. Sargeant, January 1972 (Out of print)

The Soviet Presence in the Eastern Mediterranean by Lawrence L. Whetten, September 1971 (Out of print)

The Military Unbalance: Is the U.S. Becoming a Second Class Power? June 1971 (Out of print)

The Future of South Vietnam by Brigadier F. P. Serong, February 1971 (Out of print)

Strategy and National Interests: Reflections for the Future by Bernard Brodie, January 1971 (Out of print)

The Mekong River: A Challenge in Peaceful Development for Southeast Asia by Eugene R. Black, December 1970 (Out of print)

Problems of Strategy in the Pacific and Indian Oceans by George C. Thomson, October 1970 (Out of print)

Soviet Penetration into the Middle East by Wynfred Joshua, July 1970. Revised edition, October 1971 (Out of print)

Australian Security Policies and Problems by Justus M. van der Kroef, May 1970 (Out of print)

Detente: Dilemma or Disaster? by Gerald L. Steibel, July 1969 (Out of print)

The Prudent Case for Safeguard by William R. Kintner, June 1969 (Out of print)

AGENDA PAPERS

The China Sea: The American Stake in its Future by Harold C. Hinton, January 1981

NATO, Turkey, and the Southern Flank: A Mideastern Perspective by Ihsan Gürkan, March 1980

The Soviet Threat to NATO's Northern Flank by Marian K. Leighton, November 1979

Does Defense Beggar Welfare? Myths Versus Realities by James L. Clayton, June 1979

Naval Race or Arms Control in the Indian Ocean? (Some Problems in Negotiating Naval Limitations) by Alvin J. Cottrell and Walter F. Hahn, September 1978

Power Projection: A Net Assessment of U.S. and Soviet Capabilities by W. Scott Thompson, April 1978

Understanding the Soviet Military Threat, How CIA Estimates Went Astray by William T. Lee, February 1977 (Out of print)

Toward a New Defense for NATO, The Case for Tactical Nuclear Weapons, July 1976 (Out of print)

Seven Tracks to Peace in the Middle East by Frank R. Barnett, April 1975

Arms Treaties with Moscow: Unequal Terms Unevenly Applied? by Donald G. Brennan, April 1975 (Out of print)

Toward a U.S. Energy Policy by Klaus Knorr, March 1975 (Out of print)

Can We Avert Economic Warfare in Raw Materials? US Agriculture as a Blue Chip by William Schneider, Jr., July 1974

BOOKS

Arms, Men, and Military Budgets: Issues for Fiscal Year 1981 by Francis P. Hoeber, William Schneider, Jr., Norman Polmar, and Ray Bessette, May 1980

Arms, Men, and Military Budgets: Issues for Fiscal Year 1979 by Francis P. Hoeber, David B. Kassing, and William Schneider, Jr., February 1978

Arms, Men, and Military Budgets: Issues for Fiscal Year 1978 edited by Francis P. Hoeber and William Schneider, Jr., May 1977

Arms, Men, and Military Budgets: Issues for Fiscal Year 1977 edited by William Schneider, Jr., and Francis P. Hoeber, May 1976

*   *   *

Intelligence Requirements for the 1980s: Counterintelligence (Volume III of a Series) edited by Roy Godson, January 1981

Intelligence Requirements for the 1980s: Analysis and Estimates (Volume II of a Series) edited by Roy Godson, June 1980

Intelligence Requirements for the 1980s: Elements of Intelligence (Volume I of a Series) edited by Roy Godson, October 1979

*   *   *

New Foundations for Asian and Pacific Security edited by Joyce E. Larson, September 1980

The Fateful Ends and Shades of SALT: Past . . . Present . . . And Yet to Come? by Paul H. Nitze, James E. Dougherty, and Francis X. Kane, March 1979

Strategic Options for the Early Eighties: What Can Be Done? edited by William R. Van Cleave and W. Scott Thompson, February 1979

Oil, Divestiture and National Security edited by Frank N. Trager, December 1976

Indian Ocean Naval Limitations, Regional Issues and Global Implications by Alvin J. Cottrell and Walter F. Hahn, April 1976